The New Economy of Art

Value, patronage and emerging business models in contemporary visual art

The New Economy of Art

Edited by
Gilane Tawadros and Russell Martin

This edition © DACS (Design and Artists Copyright Society) and Artquest, 2014
All individual texts and images © the artists and authors, 2014

First published in 2014 by
DACS (Design and Artists Copyright Society)
33 Old Bethnal Green Road
London E2 6AA
United Kingdom
www.dacs.org.uk

and
Artquest
University of the Arts London
272 High Holborn
London WC1V 7EY
United Kingdom
www.artquest.org.uk

Design and Artists Copyright Society is a Company Limited by Guarantee. Reg. England No. 1780482
Artquest is a programme of University of the Arts London

ISBN: 978-0-9548158-1-3

10 9 8 7 6 5 4 3 2 1

Copy Editor: Linda Schofield
Designer: SMITH;
Alice Austin, Allon Kaye, Justine Schuster
www.smith-design.com
Printed and bound in China

British Library Cataloguing in Publication Data.
A catalogue record for this book is available from the British Library.

Supported by Arts Council England's Grants for the Arts and University of the Arts London.

DACS ARTQUEST

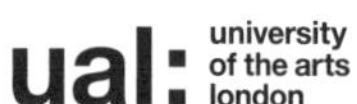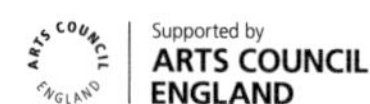

Gilane Tawadros and Russell Martin

Preface

The art world is in crisis. Artists' capacity to earn from their work is diminished; quality opportunities to make work and the funding required to support them are drying up; art schools retrench in the face of cuts even as education debts for the next generation of artists rocket skyward.

The art world is in the best shape it has ever been. Auction houses report record sales, increasing dizzyingly each season; blue chip commercial galleries and art fairs sprout like mushrooms; millions of tourists cite our museums and galleries as motivation for visiting each year; our creative education is the envy of the world.

How these vastly divergent situations can be simultaneously true is the subject of this book. Bringing together the differing perspectives of artists, economists, critics and academics, and the public and private sectors of the art world, it explores how value is differentiated between the work artists *do* and the work artists *make*. Commissioned artworks further explore and contextualise this ground: the disconnect between how artworks gain financial value even while their makers are poorly, or hardly, paid.

Many of the arguments presented here build upon a series of eponymous public debates that took place mainly in 2011 and 2012, rooting the book in recent history while updating its terms. We have included a selection of quotes from the over 300 attendees and speakers at these debates, reflecting on the changes in terrain to help understand the future.

Gilane Tawadros
Chief Executive
DACS

Russell Martin
Programme Manager
Artquest

Artists are artists and
It is society that is que
art, not the value of th
this society can be sur
allow art to happen. W
circumstances for art
what we do, because t
That's what we have t

Susan Hiller, The Economy of Art, November 2009

they make art.
stioning the value of
e artist. It's about how
e that it continues to
hat are the best
to happen? We do
hat is what we do.
o do.

Louisa Buck

What price the artist?

Never has the profile of contemporary art been so high. Museums and art galleries report escalating attendance figures; biennials, triennials and arts festivals proliferate across the globe; and the cultural and regenerative value of investing in arts institutions and conspicuous public art projects is extolled from Folkestone (UK) to Doha (Qatar). Despite an ever more volatile world economy, the market for contemporary art has also expanded both within the UK and internationally to an extent unimaginable two decades ago, with an increasing number of art fairs and widespread reports of burgeoning sales and expanding collector bases, as well as new markets in the BRIC countries – Brazil, Russia, India and China – and across the Far and Middle East.

Yet at the same time cuts in government funding for the arts in the UK, America and in many European countries have resulted in closures, redundancies and a shrinkage of contemporary arts programming and commissioning in many publicly-funded galleries. There may be an abundance of rhetoric surrounding the cultural necessity of art and intense scrutiny of the sums generated by the sale of artworks but this is not preventing the dismantling of much of the infrastructure necessary to ensure the survival of a dynamic and varied artistic ecosystem. Meanwhile, the individual artist, upon whose output the entire edifice of the current art world depends, often appears to be excluded from its transactions and activities altogether.

This publication is the result of a collaboration between Artquest and DACS (Design and Artists Copyright Society), building on a partnership of several years. For over three decades DACS has played a crucial role in supporting and sustaining artistic practice and livelihood by collecting, distributing and managing artists' royalties and artistic copyright with increasing effectiveness: £67 million has been distributed to 20,000 artists since 1984. From 2001 onwards Artquest has provided the resources, training, networks, debates and opportunities that artists require to develop their careers and understanding of the art world. A programme of University of the Arts London supported by Arts Council England, Artquest has supplied residencies, support, research and mentoring for artists, with the needs of new graduates being just as great as those with established practices.

Within a complex, turbulent and essentially artist-unfriendly environment, DACS and Artquest continue to strive to give visual artists a more prominent voice and transform their economic landscape. This mission has a particular urgency given that, contrary to popular headlines concerning celebrity artists and artworks commanding six-figure sums, the average income of an artist in the UK remains shockingly low.

A study in 2011 funded by DACS and conducted by the Centre for Intellectual Property, Policy and Management (CIPPM) at Bournemouth University reveals that the median wage for a fine artist in 2010 was £10,000 – less than half the average UK salary – with no material change in artists' earnings over the last 20 years. Overall, this survey of 5,800 British designers, fine artists, illustrators and photographers confirms the precarious financial nature of a career in the visual arts, and the unequal distribution of art market wealth, with the top 7% of visual creators earning about 40% of total income, and the remaining 93% earning the other 60%.

In order to give a more prominent voice to the marginalised maker and to gather first-hand information about the experience of today's artists, DACS and Artquest, with the Contemporary Art Society, inaugurated a series of public debates to explore the role and status of visual artists in the twenty-first century and examine how artists are functioning within this new economic climate. Panels of artists and selected specialists from within the various sectors of the art world were given the opportunity to talk freely, to air key issues and questions, and to discuss potential strategies to ensure their creative and financial survival. The information gathered from these debates provides invaluable and sometimes unexpected insights into the attitudes, aims and aspirations of today's practitioners that will hopefully help to inform policymakers in the future.

12 November 2009 **The Economy of Art**	14 February 2011 **Artists' Futures**	18 October 2011 **What Are We Worth? Artists and the Economic Crisis**	14 March 2012 **Market Matters**	13 June 2012 **Instituted by Artists**
- Alan Freeman	- Paul Bennun	- John Kieffer	- Louisa Buck	- James Early
- Paul Graham	- Sonia Boyce	- Zineb Sedira	- Kate MacGarry	- Alistair Gentry
- Susan Hiller	- Simon Faithfull	- Bob and Roberta Smith	- Matt Roberts	- John Hill
- Michael Landy	- Paul Hobson			- Elinor Morgan
- Alan Yentob	- Klaus Thymann			- Barbara Steveni

The attitude of artists towards the current expansion of the art market continues to be highly ambivalent, with the burgeoning commercial sector widely regarded as a double-edged sword, bringing both benefits and disadvantages. Despite cultural policymaker John Kieffer describing the gallery system as 'something out of the seventeenth century, never mind the twenty first', and the problematic statistic produced by curator and lecturer Matt Roberts of some 28,000 artists competing for relationships with the UK's 2,000 galleries, it was generally acknowledged across all five debates that the continued increase in galleries and art fairs has undoubtedly led to more artists being able to show and sell their work, and representation by a commercial gallery remains a major aspiration for many artists. Gallerist Kate MacGarry spoke for many in her sector when she stressed that the primary role of the gallerist is to act as an agent for artists, to assist in their development and to nurture their careers as well as to achieve sales.

Yet even artists with a substantial measure of market success also have strong misgivings about the commercial sector. There was a general consensus that an art fair is rarely a conducive environment in which to view and appreciate work, and artists Paul Graham, Susan Hiller and Michael Landy each discussed how the ever-increasing conflation of art with money is antithetical to why they make their work and how they regard it. Graham noted the disjunction between the practising artist's intense emotional engagement with their work and the cold calculations of market value; Landy recalled a feeling of 'betrayal' on the first occasion a collector put one of his artworks into auction; while Hiller expressed many an artist's concern when she bemoaned 'the vast pool of underpaid people propping up a huge superstructure of salaries'.

While the contemporary art market may constitute the most conspicuous revenue stream for artists, it is by no means their only source of income. The CIPPM study confirmed the extent to which artists are multitasking in order to make ends meet, with the majority of careers sustained by a portfolio of other activities and 35% of artists declaring a formal second job. This finding chimed across all the debates' artist panellists and audience members, including artists Sonia Boyce, Simon Faithful, Zineb Sidera and Bob and Roberta Smith, each of whom variously described how commissions, residencies and a wide range of teaching and/or lecturing jobs underpinned their art practice and provided vital funds.

An important consideration for many artists is therefore the extent to which recent cuts in public spending, the introduction of student fees for higher education and the current government's reassessment of the role of arts and humanities within the broader curriculum all pose a very real threat to these sources of artist income, as well as to the long-term condition of the creative sector in general. Boyce drew parallels with the cuts to the National Endowment of the Arts in America in the mid-1990s, and expressed concern that the impact of the current withdrawal of state patronage in the UK is privileging certain forms of art practices to the detriment of others, and giving yet more significance to the role of the private patron and to the activities of the art market. Bob and Roberta Smith also expressed the widespread fear that an increasing reliance on private philanthropy 'distorts the mission' of public institutions.

But other potentially advantageous systems have also entered the frame, most notably the internet. Of course, many practitioners are already using digital technology as a means both to create and to distribute their work, and panellists from all sectors acknowledged the current value of the internet as a recourse, a research tool and a means of mass-communication. Yet while there may be increasing numbers of online sites where artists can sell their work, in an art world that continues to be dominated by unique – or limited edition – objects and where the physical encounter with the artwork is paramount, the direct economic benefit of the internet remains unclear. Roberts counselled caution against artists being seduced by the convenience of online transactions to sell too cheaply and too soon, while Kieffer appeared to sum up the current situation by expressing the opinion that the internet 'works for some people but it doesn't work for others', with online platforms falling 'somewhere between quasi-shopping and not a very good way of looking at art'.

A more important and encouraging development seems to be the way in which the current economic status quo is encouraging the establishment of new networks and relationships. Rather than waiting passively to be 'discovered' by established commercial and/or institutional outlets, artists both within and outside the established art market are increasingly mobilising to organise exposure and potential sales for themselves. A number of panellists cited the fact that, despite the recession, there has been a growth of artist-led spaces in London and throughout the UK, some connected to artists' studios, others functioning as freestanding or pop-up showcases/project spaces, of which Temporary Arts Projects (TAP) in Southend, Outpost in Norwich, Aid and Abet in Cambridge and Platform-A in Middlesbrough are just a few examples. Roberts also observed that funding agencies and more established organisations are beginning to recognise the expanding role of artists into 'mediators, translators, facilitators for the commercial experience'.

Many of these more recent artist initiatives are specifically structured for pragmatic and creative considerations to coexist, often to the point of interchangeability. James Early of the south London-based artists' group LuckyPDF, which creates online television programmes, internet interventions and live events, described how he and his fellow members have created 'a new institutional model for delivery of art through television shows' in response to a perceived need to extend the parameters of the art world, reach new audiences and invite other artists to work outside their normal context. LuckyPDF is just one example of the effective way in which artists are using the framing device of an anonymous, quasi-institutional collective identity as a means to play with and off existing art world structures. In the process, they are both enhancing their credibility and negotiating power with larger organisations while at the same time using the aura of corporate officialdom to mask an intention that is often quite the opposite.

Another example of this significant new quasi-institutional model is Market Project, a collective initiative by eight artists based in the east of England that describes itself as an 'ongoing research project', whose main function is to collate and disseminate information on the economics of the art world, predominantly in the form of public forum events. Here the aim is not to make collaborative art, but to inform artists and encourage them to take direct control of their own career development and peer support 'beyond the usual confines of the studio group or affiliations based on artistic medium or galleries', and also, and more provocatively, to act as a whistleblower, flagging up pitfalls and citing specific examples of bad practice within the existing art world. As Market Project member and debate panellist Alistair Gentry commented, 'people don't like talking about money in the art world ... we are all practising artists but we're taking on this persona of researchers as well, and really poking our heads above the parapet ... to share our knowledge and to share our concerns.'

So while the price of the artist might currently be scandalously low, artists are becoming less prepared to accept this economic marginalisation as their lot. Artists have always been infinitely resourceful in producing the maximum output from the minimum of means and, while they may have mixed feelings about the art world in general and the art market in particular, many are becoming increasingly entrepreneurial and proactive in forging relationships among themselves and throughout the creative sector in order to make things happen on their terms. Both historically and in the current climate artists have never been given sufficient credit for their ability to operate as highly efficient micro businesses, running on the slimmest of overheads, maximising the minimum of recourses and often literally making something out of nothing.

It may be an essential human impulse to make art: in Susan Hiller's words, 'art is inevitable because some people simply have to be artists ... we do what we do, because that is what we do. That's what we have to do.' But, as these debates have confirmed, artists are now demanding that they be rewarded and not penalised for this urge, and that their value to our culture, society and especially to our economy be given due acknowledgement. For as Hiller also observes, 'if there were such a thing as a successful art strike ... I think a lot of people would be in trouble!'

Nothing's free in the art world.
It may be free to you, but
somebody paid for it: a free
public event run by the local
Council may be free to you but
somebody paid for it.

Alastair Gentry, Instituted by Artists, June 2012

I always say the more we ask for fees, the more likely we are to get them. After having done shows in different places, I can say that the UK is very stingy with artists' fees: you always have to demand them. In America I've noticed that even if you don't ask, they still give you [a fee]: it's automatic. In England, they hope you won't ask.

The art world runs on free labour and this is a huge problem for the really brilliant kid from a poor background who might not even get past the starting block. It's a matter of quality, I think, as well as quantity.

Zineb Sedira, What are we worth?
Artists and the Economic Crisis,
October 2011

Louisa Buck, Market Matters, March 2012

Alan Freeman

All our tomorrows: the irresistible economics of art for everyone

Memories of development

When celluloid passed away, a metaphor was lost. Our teachers used to tell us that when something 'developed' it went through an evolutionary process; yet the word spoke also of magical things that happened in dark rooms. In the minds of four generations who waited patiently while chemists performed secret rituals on carefully sealed rolls of film, the idea of coming into being was inextricably linked with becoming visible.

It is hard to express the full force of this duality to anyone who has not stood in a pool of dark red light while a tray of chemicals summons an image from a blank sheet. Early dawn in a campsite clearing might evoke those Rorschach moments when vague smudges coalesce into meaning, but this conveys neither the emptiness of the starting point, nor the special way that memory fired the passion to discern. 'Developing' a photograph was a craft-industrial process that reunited science and art to create what the painter, photographer and Bauhaus professor László Moholy-Nagy identified as a truly modern moment.[1] Technique and the artist collaborated to shape the uniquely expressive aesthetic that we now call black-and-white – a subgenre that defined into existence the visual experience of the newspaper age.

However, those who dreamed that some combination of state-of-the-art chemicals and precision lenses might turn us into latter-day Cartier-Bressons soon discovered that artistic excellence demanded more than handling the medium; it called for the capacity to visualise what could be recorded on it. The great photographers, whatever the mythology, did not just point and shoot. They exercised visual imagination to catch moments that materialised, in the gloom of the darkroom, as works of frozen beauty. If good economists are possible, they should be like the great photographers, seeing in the world of today those images of its future that, when developed, will reveal a beauty still invisible to contemporaries, inspiring them to will it into existence.

One is drawn to such memories when grappling with the economic philistinism of most British attitudes to arts funding. Despite enthusiasm and the occasional inspired moment, policymaking appears stuck in the age of the holiday snap. No sooner has one minister finished decapitating his subjects by framing their bellies, than the next obliterates them by sticking his finger across the lens. As for the rest of us, we sit in darkened rooms, staring at blank sheets in baths of mysterious potions, hoping something will emerge.

This text aims to cultivate the visual faculties of the nation by looking at art through a different lens. It exhibits the economics of a world in which both creative talent and aesthetic discernment are universal; in which art and science are reunited and all that remains of work is humanity; in which machinery is the servant and humans the architects. I will try to prove that such a world would grow, economically, in an altogether new way, such that human capacity uses sophisticated technology to expand along the dimension of creative, mental, social and spiritual development, while releasing us from dependence on the exhaustible resources of the earth, converting us from plunderers to custodians of our planet, curators of the natural world and explorers of the universe beyond.

This same form of growth can put humans back into a human relation with each other, recognising and properly rewarding the emancipatory worth of caring, of interdependence, of being part of a society, in which shared values, achievements, hopes and aspirations replace brute greed to lay foundations on which the true individuals of the future can confidently build the new worlds of their choosing.

Our present world displays this future to us as an undeveloped image. Creative labour is working in tandem with a new category of aesthetic demand for the products of imagination. Together they make possible a virtuous circle, an outward spiral towards a society that unleashes both the creativity and the aesthetic capabilities with which, as humans, we are born.

This future is also necessary. Mechanisation, the motor of industrial growth since 1733, has exhausted its economic potential. With only 20% of the modern workforce engaged in producing material goods, it is no longer *possible* to expand the economy by simply 'making more things'. Sustained and sustainable growth can be based only on the 80% in what we now archaically call 'services'.

Machines and technology are just as necessary, in fact more so, because only the technologies of information, communication, transport and the modern city can harness this new creative potential. The primary function of machines, however, can no longer be to reduce the human contribution to production to the minimum but, instead, must increase it to the maximum. The form of work in which we must invest is therefore creative labour, that which makes itself recognisable by setting its stamp on what it produces. The issue facing 'developers' is thus the purpose of mechanisation, which has to change not just gear but direction, serving the expansion of the human mind instead of the multiplication of material objects.

This mode of growth is also necessary right now, and not in some distant Rostowian future, for those nations where four-fifths of the world lives, that are struggling for what writer Radhika Desai terms 'industrial security', a wry analogy with 'food security', which she uses to convey the basic capability to produce the technology on which human development depends.

My aim is to open a discussion about why a world that is both possible, and necessary, is not yet developing. In place of a policy prescription that is

best produced by those on the front line of change, I hope to develop some kind
of understanding of the radical nature of the break that they will need to make.
The corridors of power will open in due course. This text is devoted to the doors
of perception.

Post-what, exactly?
Technology, humans and the political economy of creativity

Chart 1 shows the proportion of the labour force of the major industrial
countries that is working in 'services', an economic concept that, like many,
needs to be reformulated to solve our visualisation problem. The trend,
however, is so unmistakable that we will see it no matter how we frame it.
It is the same in all countries – in China, the majority of the workforce is now
employed in this sector. It is uninterrupted. It has been underway for 70 years
or more. The bulk of economically active people no longer work in what we
call manufacturing. They never will again.

In response to the early evidence of this change, the term 'post-industrial'
gained currency in the 1970s, entering mainstream discourse via Ivan Illich[2]
and then Daniel Bell.[3] Many post-industrial ideas shape the way we still think.
They painted an image of the future in which knowledge, magically separated
from knowers, will be traded like potatoes, while a creative class of experts
and superstars emerges as the new ruler of society; workers will be replaced
by robots and leisure will become the only human activity. Communications
will make cities redundant while, in more dystopic accounts, material greed
will destroy the planet unless we retreat from growth into primitive asceticism.

These ideas were once thought daring, yet the very phrase 'post-industrial'
sums up the limits of their vision. Services, in fact, comprise industries in every
sense of the word. They are branches of the division of labour, using well-
defined resources and processes to create easily identified products. They differ
in two vital respects from mechanical industries: their defining resources are
neither machines nor materials, but types of labour – caring, providing,
discovering, sustaining and creating – and their defining products are not
passive objects but bearers of human relations.

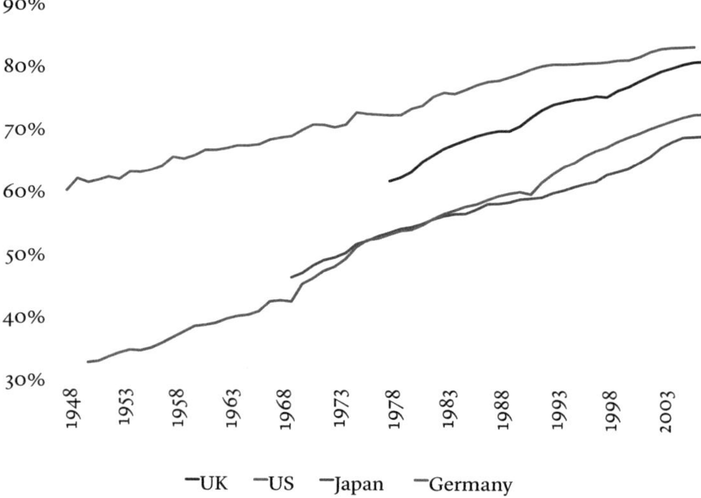

Chart 1: proportion of the workforce employed in services, major industrial countries 1948–2008

Source: Bureau of Labour Statistics, International Labour Organisation, Office for National Statistics and author calculations

Machinery, moreover, is not vanishing but is becoming vanishingly cheap, just as agricultural products have been doing for the past 300 years. Machines and devices are everywhere – in phones, buildings, transport, packaging, gadgetry – you name it, a machine is behind it. Instead of replacing labour, however, these devices are changing its nature. Labour is as overworked as ever, but has differentiated into *substitutable labour*, which can replaced by machines, and *non-substitutable labour*, which cannot. The labour of services has grown to 80% because, machinery having displaced labour continuously for 300 years, what remains is precisely that which cannot be displaced.

The result is neither a world without machines, nor a world without labour, but one in which the relation between the two has changed utterly. Along with it the function of machinery and the role of labour have also changed. The nature of the change, however, has yet to be recognised. Knowledge does not roam the world as a disembodied spirit but is embedded in human minds and applied by human hands. Our cities are more than a post-modern fusion of industrial waste heap, exotic play area and social dumping ground: they are the cradles of a potential future humanity. Taste, talent, expertise and stardom are not signs of wealth but of underdevelopment, of achievements that billions could emulate, if we could only dedicate the same resources to care, education and the cultivation of taste and talent that we now lavish on despoliation, destruction and greed.

There is no need to exhaust the resources of the planet. Using the technologies that Mark Swilling and his colleagues term 'resource-decoupling',[4] we can grow in a different way and a different direction – by expanding the mental, spiritual capabilities of humans, and focusing on the technologies that allow us to do that.

The key to the emerging new relation between people and their machinery is creative production, which, despite a history dating back to pre-industrial times, had by 1960 all but vanished from economic thinking. To understand where it went, let us first ask why it has come back.

The secret of creation

On 13 January 2014 the UK Department for Culture, Media & Sport[5] released new data for employment and output in the UK's creative industries.[6] The data dramatically confirmed the most basic feature of the creative economy: it is growing faster, in fact, than any other UK production industry. Employing 2.5 million people and accounting for 5.2% of gross value added, UK creative employment grew at an average annual rate of 2.4% compared with 0.7% overall between 2004 and 2012, a period spanning the longest and deepest recession since the 1930s.[7]

Where does this growth come from? What miracle gadget must our boffins produce for our trusty agents before the dastardly Chinese take over the creative world? None. The magic stands behind the camera. We already have the gadgetry we need, and what we do not have, our creatives will design. The secret of creation is the resource that budget after budget is paring to the bone as government after government decrees learning, talent and artistry to be a frivolous waste of public money to be cut loose from the 'nanny state': the secret is creative people. The secret of development is to invest in them.

Table 1 shows how many people work inside and outside the creative industries, as now defined by DCMS. Over a third of the 1.7 million people who work in them are 'creative specialists': the artists, architects, performers, designers, writers, publishers, broadcasters, advertisers and developers – all 888,000 of them who make the products that fuel this growth. To study what they do, the researchers who informed DCMS's updated definition coined the term 'creative intensity'[8] – the proportion of the workforce that is creatively occupied. This is shown in the last column of Table 1.

Industry	Workforce	Creative specialists	Creative intensity
Advertising and marketing	143,000	75,000	52%
Architecture	89,000	55,000	62%
Crafts	7,000	3,000	43%
Design: product, graphic and fashion	116,000	73,000	63%
Film, TV, video, radio and photography	238,000	146,000	61%
IT, software and computer services	558,000	242,000	43%
Publishing	223,000	119,000	53%
Museums, galleries and libraries	86,000	18,000	21%
Music, performing and visual arts	224,000	158,000	71%
Creative Industries Total	1,684,000	888,000	53%
Non-Creative Industries Total	27,600,000	865,000	3%

Source: DCMS 2014, Creative Industries Economic Estimates and author calculations

Table 1: creative intensity in DCMS creative industries in 2012

Creative intensity, in the creative industries as now defined by DCMS, is 17 times higher than outside them and in only three industries does it fall below 50%. Such specialisation is an exception: only 12% of workers in 'Electricity, gas, steam and air conditioning supply' industries are 'Skilled metal and electrical trades' workers, and most electricians do not work in the electricity industry. However, there are more creatives inside the creative industries (888,000) than outside (865,000).

This is completely different from traditional industries, which are not defined by who they employ but either by what they produce, as with chemicals or pharmaceuticals; by the way they produce it, as with manufacturing; or by the resources they depend on, as with mining or oil. The reason that traditional industries work this way is *mechanisation*: the replacement of living artisans by mechanical devices. Mechanisation is, to put it simply, the way we got to be where we are. It is what made the 'industrial revolution' a revolution. It was not just a technical process: it was a human and social one, as we know from experience and heartfelt pleas like Thomas Carlyle's:

Were we required to characterise this age of ours by any single epithet we should be tempted to call it, not an Heroical, Devotional, Philosophical or Moral Age, but, above all others, the Mechanical Age. It is the Age of Machinery, in every outward and inward sense of that word ... Nothing is now done directly, or by hand; all is by rule and calculated contrivance ...

On every hand, the living artisan is driven from his workshop, to make
room for a speedier, inanimate one. The shuttle drops from the fingers
of the weaver; and falls into iron fingers that ply it faster.[9]

Yet machinery did not just expel labour: it transformed labour into
appendages of itself. Henry Ford's assembly line was the apotheosis of this
process. The 'dark satanic mills' did not just expel workers but enslaved them,
converting them into a kind of inferior machine, readying them for eventual
replacement. Harry Braverman explains how traditional industry 'de-skills' its
labourers by reducing work to a series of simple, repetitive actions, ironing out
all difference between types of labour and, in so doing, removing all trace of
human influence from the results.[10]

Mechanisation worked by increasing the sheer quantity of material objects,
by factors of tens, hundreds, sometimes thousands. Its characteristic methods,
along with its language, penetrated and swamped the qualitative dimension
of change in all spheres of life. A classic case is the household gadget, which
was presented not as life-enhancing but 'labour-saving' or 'convenient'. 'Fast
food' says it all: the fridge, the cooker and the microwave did nothing to the
menu; they just let the housewife get on with her real job of raising the kids,
fuelling the husband and expanding the waistline. The measure of success
was making more for less. The driver of success was the machine.

Radhika Desai and I use the term 'Machinocratic' to describe both this age
and the outlook inherited from it. This analogy is the economic school known
as the 'Physiocrats', who believed that value came only from the land, that only
agricultural produce contained it, and that the 'unproductive' cities and towns
merely repackaged and distributed this original value. For the Machinocrats,
value comes from machines and lives in things. The 'unproductive' service
industries are a wasteful froth that plays with surface appearance to repackage
and redistribute the true value that lies in the object.

The creative economy has reversed this trend. It does not depend on a
secret formula, a killer invention or a fabulous mineral: its special resource
is its creative workforce. The very idea of a theatre without actors, or an
orchestra without musicians, makes this point. However, it is not just the
labour force that should concern us but what these labourers produce. Their
usefulness resides not in size or quantity, but in distinctiveness. The creative
economy raises its productivity in a new way: not by making more of the
same, but by adding to the variety of uses that can be made of it. This is why
it demonstrates the possibility of a society that develops by extending diversity,
instead of quantity.

The creative economy is by no means unambiguously good. As Andy Pratt and others have shown, it brings huge new problems – precarious labour, celebritisation and the cult of the superstar, new forms of hierarchy and discrimination, the merging of political and media power.[11] The list is a long one. The world that we choose to make with this new industry is as much a matter of judgement and visualisation as the image in the development bath. Yet, whatever we do with it, it sounds the death knell of the age of machines, as surely as the power loom announced the end of the age of land.

Aesthetics, distinction and the limits to quantitative growth

Late twentieth-century technology, if nothing else, has enhanced the demand for ancient Greek prefixes. It gives us unprecedented capacity to communicate, which we measure in kilohertz, ever-expanding power measured in gigawatts, storage measured in terabytes, computing speed counted in petaflops, and destructive capacities fortunately so far limited to megatons. But these magnitudes no longer help us decide what to do, because they no longer bear any obvious relation to the way we use this power. Creative production adds an entirely different dimension to that of quantity, namely, the use to which we put things.

To clarify this point I begin with the most characteristic fallacy of the mechanical age. In an early attempt to state the economic case for arts funding, the US economist William Baumol argued that an orchestra cannot 'produce more' by playing faster: the 'productivity' of the arts will therefore always fall behind the mechanical industries and so, like some Victorian poor cousin, the public purse should open to them.[12]

It is difficult to imagine a more complete way of getting everything upside down. If this vision of the service relation held true, consumers would be indifferent to everything except the length of the performance. The competence and artistic sensitivity of the performers, the excellence of the soloists or the conductor, never mind the works performed, the quality of the sound or the aura of the recital, would change nothing. They would be equally content with a night in Carnegie Hall, a bad digital rendering or a ringtone. All would just be 'performances': the only way performers could add to the happiness of the greatest number would be to play for longer, more often and louder.

This is wrong by the simplest economic criterion: it does not account for consumer behaviour. Actually, consumers make *aesthetic choices* that are, in general, specific to a group who share a preference: some like classics, and some like it hot; some go to galleries, others watch telly. Some play video games, some watch football. Moreover, this type of behaviour is growing. Every sphere of production we once thought simply quantitative is bedevilled, bewitched and bewildered by aesthetics. As Paul Stoneman points out, once upon a time car makers put a new engine under the bonnet every year. Now, they put a new bonnet over the engine.[13]

Generically, an orchestra produces 'performances', fashion designers create 'clothes', while Samsung, Apple and Sony, it is rumoured, make 'phones'. Artists make paintings and sculptures, theatres make plays and football teams make games. Baumol would have been right if, like Oliver Twist, the only thing consumers did was ask for more. In that case, their aesthetic choices would not affect total demand – only the way it is divided up. We could measure the productivity of the footwear industry in pairs per foot, and that of the music industry in notes per ear.

This is not what happens. The demand for shoes is not fixed by the number of feet in the world, nor artworks by the number of eyes. Creative consumers are willing, able and *right* to pay more for something they find aesthetically pleasing. They do this, moreover, as groups – the group of Prada-wearers, Beethoven-lovers, iPhone-users or, for that matter, residents of Hampstead, the usefulness of which shows up in postcode property factors. Beyond the generic use value of a product, an additional use is superimposed: that of being different. *Distinction*, in short, acquires a use. Creative producers create use by adding difference.

Will Page, former chief economist with PRS for Music, demonstrated how distinction itself creates a new use.[14] He and his colleagues compared sales of recorded material (CDs, discs, tapes and so on) with revenues from live performance. Conventional wisdom held that downloading would destroy the music industry because if consumers could get recordings for next to nothing they would stop paying for music. Actually they did something completely different: they spent more on live performance. They started treating it, in short, as *enhanced performance*, worth more to them than recorded performance.

Chart 2, which shows their results, definitively resolves Baumol's outdated paradox. The arts can indeed raise their productivity, by increasing the *variety* of consumer experience and, with it, the range and sophistication of the human capacities they engage.

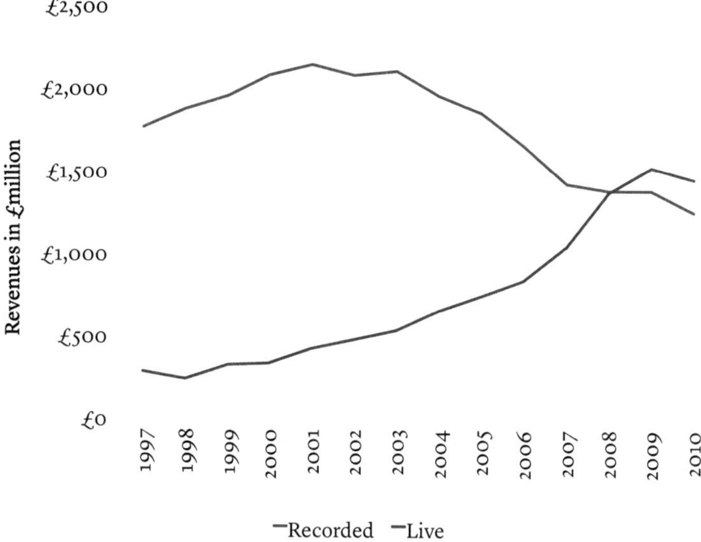

Source: PRS for Music, *Adding Up the Industry*, 2011

Chart 2: Revenue from recorded and live music in the UK, 1997–2010

Quality also redefines quantity. It is only thus that we can understand how information and communication technologies (ICT) have really affected the economy. They have achieved a revolution in service productivity – not, however, via a quantitative increase in the 'hours of service' but through the qualitative expansion of the service by the addition of distinctions.

If we look at ICT as we should any economic phenomenon, by studying what they do rather than how they do it, we see a set of technologies that are dissolving the physical bond of the traditional service relation. Part of a process stretching back to the dawn of writing, they let us reproduce the *experience* of this relation – listening, seeing, interacting, even smelling and touching – without both parties being simultaneously present. Communication technologies remove the barriers of distance whereas recording and reproduction technologies eradicate the barrier of time. At the same time reproduction technology raises the number of people involved in any interaction without any obvious limit. 'Services' can be delivered, thanks to ICT, across any distance, in any quantity and at any time.

Actually, and ironically, this has also facilitated an unprecedented quantitative increase in access to service products. An orchestra can indeed increase its 'output', even in Baumol's limited conception, by thousands and possibly millions. It can broadcast; it can record; it can webcast. The only reason this is not recognised as a productivity increase is a dim darkroom awareness that in the world now developing it is quality, not width, that counts.

The human use of human beings: the case for a new kind of growth

In a largely forgotten work, Norbert Wiener, founder of cybernetics, the study of intelligent machines, asked the awkward question, 'if machines can do everything, what are we here for?'[15] Interest in this topic started with the still-earlier question, 'how can we tell a machine from a human?' To answer it, computing pioneer Alan Turing devised a fiendish test that unwittingly presaged the age of Twitter. In it, a machine and a human interact through text. The human can ask any question and must guess from the answers whether a machine or a human is at the other end. If it was impossible to tell the difference, a machine would qualify as humanoid.

The theme recurs iconically in Fritz Lang's *Metropolis* (1927) and in Ridley Scott's *Blade Runner* (1982), the film version of Philip K. Dick's superbly prophetic *Do Androids Dream of Electric Sheep* (1968). The difference between the two expresses the entire issue. Lang supposes a mechanical human, a 'second Maria' copied from real life by a crazed inventor – interestingly, the model for Dr Strangelove, down to the leather glove on an uncontrollable prosthetic right hand. The second Maria is visually and corporeally human, but her mechanical being incarnates every conceivable concept of evil: she is Jezebel, the Antichrist, lust and moral abandon, combined in a single figure whose greatest sin is to be invented instead of conceived. We are not expected to shed a single tear when she is literally burned to death by a crazed mob.

Philip K. Dick's androids, in contrast, turn out to be more human than people. They yearn to understand the value of life, which they cling to with a greater passion than those who granted it, in the desolate hope that the creatures who wished them into existence might give them some insight into its purpose by allowing them to qualify as co-equals.

The asymmetry of Turing's test gives the game away. His human has to work out if there is a machine at the other end; his machine is never asked if it is talking to a human. The fear that machines will advance enough to become human is an unconscious inversion; it is frightening only because, for 300 years, industrial capitalism has grown by reducing humans to machines.[16] This accounts, I believe, for the utopic anti-industrialism of most post-industrial literature (see, for example, *The Post-Industrial Utopians* by Boris Frankel[17]). Overwhelmed and alienated by its own creations, the human race is consumed with retrieving what its own machines have stolen from it. Even artistic currents that embraced industrialism, such as Futurism, succumbed to aesthetics in which the mechanical attributes of speed, power, size and deadliness were worshipped as superior and thus antithetical to our own being.

This insight finally allows us to place creative labour in its historic context. Economically, it is labour for which a machine cannot substitute. It is a particular type of non-substitutable labour that actively resists mechanisation, as explained at greater length in *A Dynamic Mapping of the Creative Industries in the UK* by Bakhshi et al.[18] It is non-repetitive, problem-solving, inventive labour, which works to a goal rather than a plan. Starting from incomplete descriptions of what is required, it can 'produce what the customer wants' in a slightly different way each time. There are many reasons to suppose that this kind of ability cannot be reproduced by a mechanical device, which is to say a device that functions by simply repeating itself.[19]

Yet all 'service' labour is to a degree non-substitutable by virtue of its humanity. Interacting with humans is desired and sought after by other humans because we are social animals. It may be theoretically possible to incubate babies in laboratories as in Aldous Huxley's dystopic *Brave New World* (1932), but actually we prefer the old-fashioned way, not because we have to, but because we want to. For the same reason, the high end of every service industry is the one that gives the most personal service, from gourmet restaurants to chauffeur-driven cars.

It is the intrinsic preference of humans for other humans that divides the world of material products into those whose primary function is to be the bearer of the creative labour that went into them, and those where the material form determines the use. This is obvious in art forms like paintings, which are purchased not for the canvas, but because the image that it carries speaks directly of the artist who produced it. But in essence this is no different from what is happening to industries like publishing – recently reclassified as a service – or sound recording. Consumers are indifferent, basically, to whether a song is on a tape, a CD, vinyl or the internet, as long as the audio quality meets a required standard. The material cost is vanishingly small and the material is irrelevant: we pay for the performance that it carries. In a subtler way, this is why hand-crafted objects are usually more highly prized than mass-produced ones.

A general rule is at work here. The aesthetic element of every product is the evidence of the human labour that produced it: hence the cult of the signature and the Western obsession with 'originality'. This, finally, is what lies behind the 'aestheticisation' of domain after domain of material production. From cars to signature office blocks, from bathroom fixtures to Starbucks coffee cups, creatives supply objects that display, in their form and design, the care and thought that has gone into them.

This redivision of material production is telling us something about the very word 'service', whose semantic proximity to 'servant' betrays its feudal origins in the notion of direct personal attendance. The real issue is the aesthetic content, properly understood as the degree to which the special character of the labour involved in producing something determines the use that the consumer makes of it; that is, the degree to which quality predominates over quantity. The counterpart to supply of creative labour is *aesthetic demand*, which, if we wish to develop the faculty of economic visualisation, we should recognise as the capacity to understand, and appreciate, the special characteristics of the labour in any product, be it material or intangible. The key to creative growth is to expand this capacity: that is, art for everyone.

It is time to print the positive. Like any good economist, let us ask how the supply and the demand match up. We have in front of us a growth path that can expand the economy by expanding its human-ness, not by abolishing the machines but by entering a new partnership with them – actually, by humanising them. This same growth path can bring to a halt the exhaustion of the planet's resources because we can grow qualitatively, by making more and better distinctions, instead of just using more to make more. We can decrease our use of material resources at the same time that we increase our capacity to be human. Not only that, there is no other way, because the replacement of labour by machinery has exhausted itself as an economic process. The economic case is irresistible. What remains to be explained is the source of resistance.

Back to civilisation: the real limits to growth and the real case for the arts

The cruellest illusion of the mechanical age is the notion that creativity, and aesthetic discrimination, are states of higher being, luxuries that we can afford only when all material wants are satisfied, and until then reserved for an elite, a fortunate (or, in the Romantic version, 'gifted') minority. Though persistent and widespread, this illusion conflicts with the most basic facts known to anthropologists, historians and educators. A short catalogue of the things it cannot explain would be cave painting, jazz, tribal art, El Sistema and onion riots. Creativity and aesthetics are universal human capacities, products of the social character of human existence, which is why artistic activity is so central in allegedly 'primitive' hunter-gatherer societies; it is the social glue that makes material production possible. This is also why economies like China give such high priority to the creative industries, not as an alternative to climbing out of poverty, but as the means to achieve it.

It is the age of mechanisation that has deprived us of this birthright, suppressing it and reducing it to the minimum possible. All the characteristic counterpositions of our age are consequences of this separation, including the severing of art from science. In this light, however, we have to understand what 'culture' is: a creation of the mechanical age. Our forebears expelled from the factory all the non-mechanical human activities that reproduce our society, exiling them to a twilight zone that we enter only when the whistle blows. Culture is a doomed word: it is defined as non-productive. It equates to unnecessary, lazy and wasteful.

To spend money on it is, by its own self-definition, to divert resources that should be used to make 'real stuff'.

Alongside the notion of culture as wasteful and luxurious, we also find the idea that it is the province of an elite and therefore a mark of privilege. This goes back to its roots in German Romanticism where it was expressly counterposed to 'civilisation',[20] a reaction against the aristocratic rigidity of a society for which birth, expressed in 'manners and customs', was the hallmark of distinction. This gave it a very specific concept of the individual as a person 'apart' from society, a genius, a unique and indeed semi-divine creator[21] – and is one of the reasons that the Western concept of intellectual property is so fixated on the notion of origination. Two vital dimensions are missing from this *Weltanschauung*, transmitted almost unchanged into English discourse by the Romantic poets such as Samuel Taylor Coleridge:[22] the notion of universal creativity, and the concept that it is society that develops the individual, not vice versa.

Beside these conceptual and cultural obstacles, there are material ones. It is precisely because culture is the business of humans that it is difficult to invest in, especially for private funders. On the supply side, productive capacity is embedded in the creative person, the outcome of years of education, training or the simple cultivation of talent. Why should an investor pay for five years of human development, only to have it stand up and walk out?

On the demand side, the aesthetic dimension of use lacks a characteristic of material goods known as 'excludability', which is essentially what makes ownership technically possible. A traditional owner's investment is protected not just legally but physically to the extent that only one person can use a material object at a time. Texts, images and performances, in contrast, can be distributed almost without limit at vanishing cost. More disconcertingly, even material objects are losing excludability. By the miracle of fashion, a high-street buyer can indeed walk a mile in a supermodel's shoes – because it is the label, not the sole and heel, that determines the use to which the customer puts it.

By its nature, therefore, aesthetic discrimination is intrinsically collective – we 'prefer' a particular kind of art, or music or, indeed, a football team or a rock star, not just for what the work stirs in our romantic souls, but because of all the other romantic souls that share our passion. An audience is present in every act of artistic appreciation, even if only as a Lacanian absent signifier. The function of most institutions of intellectual property, including even the humble ticket, is therefore 'allocative' rather than 'productive'. They channel streams of income derived from collective consumption back to the original creative producers. Unfortunately, the natural inclination of the private owner is to channel these streams to himself, which risks choking off what is really required: a guaranteed living for the producers.

All the above make the construction of a case for funding the arts a daunting one; the advocate, it would appear, must not only overcome the natural hesitancy of the private investors, not to mention their traditional hostility to anything that smacks of higher taxes or spending public money, but must also overcome the hostility to cultural development which is built into the whole set-up that defines culture as a wasteful, non-productive, elite luxury. Can this resistance be overcome?

The first critical mental step is to grasp that the emergence of the creative economy inverts the case for funding. An investment in civilisation – not just in the technologies that make creative labour possible, but in the labour itself – is not a diversion from production but the primary prerequisite of growth. The economy of the future needs its arts and culture, because that is what the economy of the future will produce, and that is what the consumers of the future will buy. 'Culture' is not an alternative to wealth creation: it is what wealth creation, in its new form, consists of.

Even such a revolutionary rethink does not complete the picture. An adequate vision of the future calls for an answer to the question, 'what are the limits to this growth?' On the supply side, the answer has to be the number of people who are allowed to create. Expansion will be limited by the extent to which we acknowledge, and foster, the creative potential latent in every human without exception, that is, the extent to which we can build a society of creators. But this has equal implications on the demand side. If the products of this labour are to find consumers, then these same consumers must be able to consume them.

Every great surge of innovation gives rise to its characteristic new forms of consumption – the age of steam initiated passenger travel, Fordism produced car drivers, and the Golden Age gave birth to nations of gadget owners. In every case, something that was once the privilege of a small, wealthy elite was extended to a great mass of people, creating the demand that drove the expansion of supply. If the characteristic form of consumption is culture, then the *appreciation* of art has to take huge strides forward. This is not, moreover, a passive process. Indispensible to the appreciation of art is the knowledge of how it is done. The 'Three Rs' of the twenty-first century are the design, production and performance of beauty.

We can finish on a note of hope because this programme works with the grain of history, not against it. To the 'natural' unity of non-mechanical production and aesthetic appreciation we can add the following: every producer is also a consumer. An immense broadening of the 'right to culture', and an abandonment of the outdated concept of culture as an elite luxury, is no utopian post-industrial dream, but opens the door to an unprecedented expansion of both the economy and everything that defines us as human. The one thing missing is political will and courage: if artists and economists work together, they can supply the vision that may yet inspire it.

1   Oliver A.I. Botar, *Technical Detours: The Early Moholy-Nagy Reconsidered* (New York: Art Gallery of the CUNY Graduate Center, 2006)

2   Ivan Illich, *Tools for Conviviality* (London: Marion Boyars Publishing, 2001 [1973])

3   Daniel Bell, *The Coming of Post-Industrial Society* (New York: Harper Colophon Books, 1974)

4   Mark Swilling, *Growth, Resource Decoupling and Productivity* (Stellenbosch: Stellenbosch University / Geneva: United Nations Environment Programme, 2005), <www.learndev.org/dl/BtSM2011/Africa%20Policy%20Brief.pdf>

5   DCMS, *Classifying and Measuring the Creative Industries: Consultation on Proposed Changes* (London: DCMS, 2013), gov.uk/government/uploads/system/uploads/attachment_data/file/203296/Classifying_and_Measuring_the_Creative_Industries_Consultation_Paper_April_2013-final.pdf

6   DCMS, *Creative Industry Estimates* (London: DCMS, 2014), https://www.gov.uk/government/publications/creative-industries-economic-estimates-january-2014

7   NESTA, 'How Big are the UK's Creative Industries?', NESTA blog, Tuesday 14 February 2014, http://www.nesta.org.uk/blog/how-big-are-uk%E2%80%99s-creative-industries-part-3

8   Hasan Bakhshi, Alan Freeman and Peter Higgs, *A Dynamic Mapping of the Creative Industries in the UK* (London: NESTA, 2013), p.31, https://www.academia.edu/5538116/A_Dynamic_Mapping_of_the_UKs_Creative_Industries

9   Thomas Carlyle, 'Signs of the Times' ['The Mechanical Age'], *Edinburgh Review*, vol.xlix, 1829, p.439

10 Harry Braverman, *Labor and Monopoly Capital, The Degradation of Work in the Twentieth Century* (New York: New York University Press, 1998)

11 Andy C. Pratt, 'New Economy: A Cool Look at the Hot Economy', in Peter W. Daniels, Jonathan Beaverstock, Michael J. Bradshaw, and Andrew Leyshon (eds), *Geographies of the New Economy* (London: Routledge, 2006)

12 William J. Baumol and William G. Bowen, *Performing Arts, The Economic Dilemma: A Study of Problems Common to Theater, Opera, Music, and Dance* (New York: Twentieth Century Fund, 1966)

13 Paul Stoneman, *Soft Innovation: Economics, Product Aesthetics, and the Creative Industries* (Oxford: Oxford University Press, 2010)

14 Will Page, Chris Carey, Jonathan Haskel and Peter Goodridge, 'Wallet Share', *Economic Insight*, issue 22, 18 April 2011 (London: PRS for Music), http://prsformusic.com/creators/news/research/Documents/Economic%20Insight%2022%20Wallet%20Share.pdf

15 Norbert Wiener, *The Human Use of Human Beings* (Cambridge, MA: DaCapo Press, 1951)

16 Science fiction writer Iain M. Banks has created a compelling vision of a 'Culture' shared by sentient machines and humans.

17 Boris Frankel, *The Post-Industrial Utopians* (Madison, Wisconsin: University of Wisconsin Press, 1986)

18 Hasan Bakhshi, Alan Freeman and Peter Higgs, *A Dynamic Mapping of the Creative Industries in the UK* (London: NESTA, 2013), p.22, https://www.academia.edu/5538116/A_Dynamic_Mapping_of_the_UKs_Creative_Industries

19 See Alan Freeman, *Culture, Creativity and Innovation in the Internet Age*, 2008, http://ideas.repec.org/p/pra/mprapa/9007.html

20 Norbert Elias, *The Civilizing Process* (Oxford: Blackwell, vol.1 1969, vol.2 1982)

21 Rüdiger Safranski, *Schiller oder Die Erfindung des Deutschen Idealismus* (Munich: Carl Hanser Verlag, 2004)

22 Raymond Williams, *Culture and Society* (London: Hogarth Press, 1982 [1958])

Acknowledgements

Among the many people that have inspired, provoked or contributed to ideas that have taken shape in the 12-year journey, special mention goes to Hasan Bakhshi, Oliver Botar, Judith Burns, Alexander Buzgalin, Victoria Chick, Tony Clayton, Stuart Cunningham, Radhika Desai, Chris Freeman, John Hawkes, Peter Higgs, Graham Hitchen, Meng Jie, Randy Joynt, Andrew Kliman, Tom Knight, Ken Livingstone, Bengt-Ake Lundvall, Alexander Mickelthwaite, Richard Naylor, Kate Oakley, Paul Owens, Carlota Perez, Andy Pratt, Matthieu Prin, Bridget Rosewell, John Ross, Trudy Schroeder, Martin Smith, Thom Sparling, Iris Stefansdottir, Paul Stoneman, Sarah Thelwall, David Throsby and Jude Woodward. Any errors are my own.

I'd like to think about the artists that are coming out of college. Do you think that maybe the market is actually saturated now with artists, and that there are just not enough collectors out there to keep it going?

The art schools are bursting: people are coming from all over the world and paying a lot of money to go to art school, and maybe there isn't room for everyone. We're all fighting over the same collectors, but maybe this isn't the way forward for [the] survival of artists; we have to find new models.

The momentum behind the establishment of not-for-profit artist-run spaces, since 2004, gives me cause for some optimism. ... artists are getting more nimble about setting up studio and exhibition spaces: ... CoExist in Southend, Aid & Abet in Cambridge, Trove in Birmingham and Platform A in Middlesbrough. ... I think this new generation are particularly interesting because artists are coming together in a professional way without looking overly slick and commercialised. They interface with local markets; ... [and] with other arts groups and individual artists. A lot of these spaces specialise or have a particular sympathy towards multimedia, installation [and] performance, which are not so market-friendly. The market pays lip service to these art forms, but ... it privileges a certain kind of art practice.

Louisa Buck, Market Matters, March 2012

Frieze has changed the landscape of London. I mean we call it *Frieze* week now, and it brings international attention to London, but it can be quite a difficult time to have an exhibition, if you are not Gagosian or Hauser & Wirth. It is so distracting that actually it can be overwhelming. It's a bit like having lunch with 50 people and trying to have a good conversation with all of them.

Kate MacGarry, Market Matters, March 2012

Over the last couple of years, there seems to be an increased interest in how to gain representation. I'm not sure what underlies that trend; maybe it's a loss of faith in public funding with so much funding being reduced. Maybe there has always been, or at least in recent times, a lack of education or lack of awareness about the commercial sector; it remains mysterious and opaque, and artists have never really known how to benefit from it.

Matt Roberts, Market Matters, March 2012

The gallerist's job is not that different from the artist's in that the people that you meet along the way can become more and more important as things develop. The people I met on the first week of opening the gallery are still very much part of my picture. I do believe that it's all about personal relationships: art fairs have facilitated that, because not only do sales take place, but museum shows can be agreed at an art fair.

I don't think art has anything to lose by saying 'the valuation of the market is wrong, the valuation of the funders is wrong'. Why don't we try and put a value on what we're doing in consultation with our public?

Kate MacGarry, Market Matters, March 2012

Alan Freeman, The Economy of Art, November 2009

Andrew Wheatley and Andrea Phillips
in conversation with Keir McGuinness

Contemporary art and transactional behaviour

Keir McGuinness is a management consultant who for the past 14 years has specialised in working with galleries, artists and creative businesses. Andrea Phillips is professor of fine art in the Department of Art at Goldsmiths. Since 1992 Andrew Wheatley has been co-director of Cabinet Gallery, London. Andrew and Andrea, collaborating with colleagues Sarah Thelwall and Suhail Malik, are currently developing research on 'The Aesthetic and Economic Impact of the Art Market'. Working in partnership with a number of organisations including DACS, this research aims to measure the impact of the contemporary art market on publicly-funded gallery exhibition policies, artists' careers and national funding policy decisions through the analysis of primary market data. Such research has never been carried out systematically before but is critical now as the public arts sector relies ever more heavily on building commercial relationships. Through analysing what these are and how they shape what art we see and where we see it, the aim of the research is to both enhance economic and cultural understanding and contribute towards evidence-based policymaking. As part of this research, the following conversation between Phillips, Wheatley and McGuinness investigates the ways in which forms of 'transactional behaviour' are shaping the art market and its relation with public institutions both negatively and unsustainably. The conversation took place in March 2014 in London.

Andrea Phillips How did you meet each other?

Keir McGuinness We met as part of the new experience of me being asked by a long-standing client to advise him in better understanding and purchasing contemporary art. Prior to that it had been a pleasant distraction.

Andrew Wheatley But even earlier, Keir, you visited Cabinet early in our history.

KM I did, because it was so interesting. Cabinet was just completely off the wall. Almost indifferent to commercial demands.

Business magnates and philanthropists Charlie Munger and Warren Buffett have recently said that they now organise their lives with fewer distractions and make fewer decisions. I think that's just spot on. You don't have to carry out this perpetual transactional behaviour; you can look and assess and value. Unless we go back to this, trusting our experience, we will have a shallower, weaker pond.

AP Is there something about art transactions that brings this to the fore?

KM Yes. If art was in a regulated market, part of its business would be illegal
-- often one can sense the subtle manipulation of markets (which takes place
among the cognoscenti) so that the innocents don't get into it until they're
paying many times more than the initial purchase price. Individuals who
collect with their ears, who all circulate among their own selves and who
sell to themselves are apparent in the current market.

AW And if I think back to the time I met Keir, Cabinet was concerned with forging
an entity that, while we didn't necessarily know how it was going to be shaped,
was certainly predicated on appetites. It was satisfying intellectual and aesthetic
appetites, often through things that we apprehended as quite pagan or difficult.

AP Your own appetites?

AW Absolutely our own. It's one factor that I would not diminish or underrate
even now, 20 years on. Back in the early '90s it happened to coincide with Keir's
looking and the fact that we were introducing precisely what Keir described ...
to literally see something new, something unfamiliar and indeed, as Cabinet
evolved, what we were establishing was something that was quite distinctive
from other operations. You must remember, in the early days, while I might
have straddled public and private sectors, it was done without huge monetary
resources. The only capital we had was that of our minds, our eyes and certain
self-taught learning.

KM As far back as 1994 it was apparent that certain galleries were going to
be major players in the then emerging contemporary art scene, both from the
way they worked the media and through their grasp of the importance of brand
creation. This influence, on the manner in which contemporary art is now sold,
has produced what might be called the 'retailisation' of art; it's just one huge
superstore. One of the most successful auction houses in the world is owned
by a clothes retailer, while another is owned by a group of individuals who are
property businessmen. These businesses have huge budgets, which they apply
with very skilled management discipline.

AP So why are you still involved in it, given that it's in this moribund state?

KM To me it's still interesting because I like to see beautiful and interesting
objects that are hugely underappreciated ... and ... I enjoy the hunt. Every
time I go to the Basel Art Fair, I end the day desperate for a long walk away

from the place. Occasionally you find one or two interesting things that you didn't know existed, but the rest of it, thousands and thousands of objects, doesn't interest me.

AW I have an historic disinterest in secondary dealing. We accept it where it's relevant because one of our artist's works comes up in auction, or a collector turns to me and says, 'Look, I want to sell this piece', but then my vested interest, my stake, is significant. If I look back on the history of trading, traders and art dealers, there are those that are conspicuous because they've supported their trading activities through secondary dealing and we know who they are. In fact, most of my competitors in London were involved with that kind of transaction right from the get-go. A whole area of discussion opens up here in relation to secondary and primary markets. They're more porous than they've ever been – would you agree with that, Keir?

KM That's to do with control, of course.

AP What do you do if a client or somebody that's collected your artist's work says I want to sell it on the secondary market?

AW We'll try and place it, as best as we can.

AP You'll first of all try and convince them not to?

AW Well, not really … but I don't want their ambivalence to turn into a sort of reckless behaviour. And, of course, their impulse is what is its monetary value – is its monetary value greater than its cultural value? Is that proven by the records at auction houses? Yes. 'I won't go back to the primary dealer I bought it from, I will just put it on the market.' We have artists within our roster for whom that is more true than others.

KM One of the things that would really change the dynamics of the whole set-up is to somehow restrain the sale of primary art purchases for a period of, let's say, five years from the date of their purchase. In other words, if you don't sell an object that you bought and you keep it for more than, say, five years, or seven years, then you will pay less capital gains tax than those who dispose of their works in a shorter period. That's one way you can give people incentives to change their behaviour.

AP You're suggesting regulation.

KM Yes. Regulation. As a former corporate lawyer, I was from time to time involved with the Stock Exchange, where one had to observe every conceivable rule and control mechanism. When I came into art, it was extraordinary. I realised that people could transfer millions of pounds in a day (less so now) across several borders, and without any real accountability. Things changed and Customs & Excise people, some years ago, began to employ arts graduates so as to arrive at informed and intelligent decisions at the point of entry into or exit from the UK.

Several years ago, I understand that in at least one Latin American country a similar situation developed. The wealthy were buying works of art in auction, importing them into the purchaser's country of residence and paying little or no purchase tax. All of a sudden, the world changes, the economy takes off, they start paying decent salaries to their civil servants and the authorities start behaving properly and becoming more thorough. Regulation is inevitable if for no other reason than that the contemporary art market now involves the transfer of so much value across borders.

AP Would you both support forms of regulation?

KM Of course, why not? Fourteen years ago it was suggested at a national institution that a forum be set up whereby the West's accountants, lawyers, art advisors and so forth all got together and met maybe once every two years and presented papers as to how they dealt with the taxation revenues that can be gained from the trade which is art. This suggestion was purely to ensure the building up of collections in public. I may be wrong but I don't believe that anything significant has been done to take this idea forward.

Some countries do get this somewhat better than others. America has progressed; Germany has a very good grasp of it. Governments need to keep each other informed as to the processes and systems that they apply to this particular market.

AW If you look at the taxation points of my trading transactions, they're considerable. I don't set out to avoid tax, that is not a primary consideration, but I'm certainly interested in it as defined by that relationship between state and commerce. Firstly, if the public sector continues to moan about not winning key arguments at the Treasury table or with the Department for Culture, Media & Sport (DCMS), it's partly because it doesn't have the data (which our research will hopefully redress).

Secondly, the government, in terms of its economic audits, doesn't have an index dedicated to contemporary art; at the moment it's lumped in with antiquities and fashion. They don't even comprehend the growth of the art market over the last ten years, which has been considerable and rapid.

KM I suspect that were one to sit in the Treasury rooms (which I've never done), one might be surprised at the indifference directed towards the business of art. In this country art is an elitist activity; anything that is elitist is a little questionable and as such not a topic that people want to pursue politically.

AP While on the other hand government might understand the symptoms of cultural phenomena in terms of footfall at the Tates, and footfalls around most of the galleries in the UK, they haven't made that key relationship with the economy by which that's born.

KM Correct. If they say they have, they don't react accordingly.

AW Another way of illustrating this is that Tate's resources will be directed towards front-end, public-facing activity, but in terms of the back end at the moment, there's a huge poverty of resources. Works are acquired with limited funds and cannot be conserved. Supporting collections, archives: there's a diminishing budget there. The consequence of Keir's earlier remark about the absence of an effective taxation system is that institutions like the Tate now have to run around the world creating collection funds.

KM Then there's the national lottery and the funds, billions, which have been used to set up institutions that now have insufficient funds to run them.

AP The Arts Council experimented with encouraging organisations to set up an endowment.

AW They did encourage this, but I think it faltered because it wasn't properly advised. It was utilising and drawing on the free investment market without sufficient knowledge.

KM Endowments are very difficult things, in this country, because we do not endorse them, in the same way that we don't endorse giving – giving is a novelty. You have to give people incentives that are financial. If you go to people and you say 'If you do this, this benefit financially will come from it' and you can point to where those financial benefits will go in society, in the general sense of the word, it's much more palatable because people sense that they're participating, they're going to get something back. That helps enormously but that seems to be something that is completely at odds with the way the Treasury thinks.

AP Isn't there a specific problem when it comes to making that argument around art and the division that currently exists between the art market and perceptions of public institutions?

KM You will find that because it is still an elitist activity and because it is patronised by an elite, it is something different, it is something slightly more rarefied. But if you can boil it down and show demonstrably how much money will go to X or Y or Z, for whatever reason, be it the postponement of a death duty or whatever, then people will start to pay attention because the industries around it – the accountants, the lawyers, etc. – all start to show interest. Anybody who can come along and demonstrate there is a new sector to be developed will get people piling in and once you've got people piling in, you get the followers. But if you just say, oh, it's because it's socially acceptable, it's required, it's proper, it's whatever it is – forget it.

You have to demonstrate that when you put ten in, you get 14 back.

AP Of course, but there's a huge resistance to that within arts institutions, which would see that as a form of, I don't know, the instrumentalisation of fundamental freedoms.

KM When you watch the public galleries falling apart because they can't even open a quarter of their collections to anybody at any one time, when you see the artists not generating sales, then it will be interesting to see what happens thereafter. The reason secondary marketing is becoming appropriate is because many artists now have several galleries, each of which has an insufficient amount of material to take to several of the 103 art fairs that now operate annually and at which up to 70% of their sales are derived. One might be tempted to say that galleries presently maintain substantial exhibition spaces in order to placate the demands of the artists rather than as a place from which to sell the art.

It's about control of supply. If you can't control the supply at the primary level, you have to devise methods of making money somewhere else. Secondary dealing is potentially more successful at directing such supply.

AP So there's an inevitable shift towards secondary dealing.

KM Indeed, because of the way the primary market is working.

AW I'd go further than that; I'd say that primary market activities are now forged within secondary markets. Look at the auction houses in the Far East. There is no provenance for much of the art. That market exists in a vacuum. It doesn't relate to any critical assessment beyond the country in which the auction has taken place. So, actually primary markets are being circumnavigated immediately, instantaneously, by secondary auction houses.

AP How do you respond as a London-based dealer?

AW If anything it tempers my resolve to carry on what we're doing. In some ways, I can say it's an irrelevance … you adapt. The purpose of our move to a new gallery in Vauxhall is directly related to this. It is a follow-through of our own trajectory; it's as symbolic as it is anything. What's interesting about successive exhibitions is they continue to be important for the constituency of artists, particularly in London, who come through the gallery and see things that have been well articulated, as much as it helps us understand the nature of the art we're showing.

KM But you're a niche business, that's the whole point …

AP As opposed to the Gagosian Gallery, which is not niche?

AW Sure, but we also define each other … It's true to say that in terms of, I suppose, signification, the Cabinet Gallery constitutes a collective intelligence that builds through its history of interrelated activity. Exhibitions also give residual comfort to a certain generation of collectors who think one of the important elements and provenances is that Cabinet maintains a physical space.

KM It's the physical ability to be able to stand in front of an object, as opposed to an entire future generation who are solely going to prefer to view online.

AP That's not necessarily a market-driven argument though, is it?

KM No, it's not; it's counter-cyclical.

AW Of course, the other thing to bear in mind is the extraordinary tendency for more physical property to be acquired either through purchase or commercial let for display – how many thousand square metres has Gagosian got in London now?

KM They're alternative contemporary municipalities, basically, which give an experience of a museum but from which you can purchase.

AW Exactly. It's the mimicry of retailing.

AP It's mimicry of a public institution as well. But, this question about whether one has the autonomy – for instance, the idea of presenting autonomous objects: it's something very different for a public institution to do that.

KM That's why endowments are going to become very important in the future ... hopefully because they're going to be able to preserve the authority of the place, where they will not solely be dependent upon the public requirement either on the basis of popular taste or financial turnover. I understand it, but it's also very 'flattening', i.e. two dimensional/limited.

The Chisenhale Gallery, for example, is doing something very interesting because it shows artists time and time again who the collector wants. The artists use it as a place for incubation where they exhibit before they go on to other, greater things. It's the success of the place and it's the ethos of the place, but it costs.

AP Is it sustainable? And what happens to galleries like Cabinet if, as you say, the prediction is that in X years the current model becomes defunct or redundant?

KM There will be different activities undertaken, as indeed is the case today, but much more distinctively. There will be different activities undertaken by different galleries. Different galleries will perform different functions.

There is a movement forward, which is the merging, and you must have heard this so many times, of the commercial into the institute and the institute into the commercial. But it's not going to work if you merge two big things: Tate with, say, Gagosian in a joint venture would, I suspect, fail. When it comes to contemporary art there has to be something incubator-like about what goes into a public institution.

AW At every level, the commercial gallery dealer is required to put money into exhibitions of their artists, whatever age, wherever they are in their career. The monetary resource that public institutions look at tapping is the profit of the commercial gallery.

Whereas the Institute of Contemporary Arts (ICA) might have six or ten years ago dispatched some sort of commercial agreement, or consignment note, that required flat percentage commissions of 25%, I can't recall in the last few years an institution in Europe, America or in the UK that didn't require me to actually

consider putting in cash, whether it was tied to a commission on sale,
or recoupment at the point of sale or production upfront.

KM The decision of whether a gallery will take a show or not depends upon
whether you will make a financial contribution and the person who makes the
largest financial contribution gets the shows, which in my opinion is when the
'flattening' of quality can creep in.

AP But this is not just in exhibitions in publicly-funded galleries; this is also
the story of supposedly publicly-funded biennials.

KM It goes back to this question of endowment. If every significant institution
that is public has access to a state endowment, that would give them the authority
to be able to show what they wanted (almost) and survive and concentrate on
what it is they're good at rather than fundraising, at which they're not always
so commercially successful. It doesn't have to be individual; you could group
the organisations and you could create an endowment that is shared.

AW What constitutes the relationship between state and commerce, and why
is the institution (as therapeutic as it's been in the past) able to go to the
commercial dealer and ask for finance? This needs to be better structured.

KM Endowment isn't about maintaining the structure, nor is it about maintaining
the capital project, it's purely about the intellectual and aesthetic exercise of what
goes on within the building. There's no point in having a building that you can
maintain but in which you can't show anything.

AW It also presupposes that it knows what its function has been historically
and could be in the future. It goes back to actually understanding what value
the institution can ascribe to the object, and therefore the artist, that the
commercial gallery dealer cannot.

KM You're talking about the potential of partnerships between commercial
galleries, of different types, to provide different services to certain institutions
with which they're a quasi-partner.

AW No, I'm not thinking about a collaboration or relationship – I'm talking
about an understanding of what their function has been historically. I don't
think that's adequately understood.

AP Are you suggesting that, without that historical understanding, partnership can't go forward?

AW Yes.

AP Because there's an understanding that somehow the commercial sector should implicitly want to support the public institutions.

AW I mean there's a reason; it's implicit but it hasn't been made explicit. It needs to be.

I remember when I was trying to kick off this postgrad degree course in the contemporary art market – it's history, economics and business – and I recall a certain nervousness among public institutions, not least the public gallery hosting the course, because it threatened to expose those dynamics and ecologies that might serve the institution well, serve the commercial dealer and ultimately the artist, but would actually make those relationships explicit through examination and analysis.

KM Until very recently the contemporary art market was not significant enough, and did not generate significant revenues. There was an insufficient income to entertain or engage the larger government ... the larger bureaucracy. The moment one starts to get something that is akin to an 'oil' revenue, then in the absence of anything else, people go for it ... develop and take an interest in it.

What of course government will, in all probability, do if they are not careful, is they'll either miss the boat or sink it. Probably both. Or they'll kill it by over-regulation in a way that simply causes the market to go somewhere else because it's cheaper and less regulated.

In my book it only starts to be interesting when it starts to generate significant revenues. When it becomes valuable to the revenue of the country, then it becomes an issue that has to be looked at harder and that's why the instigation of some form of 'talking shop', where people once every couple of years come together and present papers and exchange ideas on particular topics, is so interesting. This approach seems to me to be sensible and much more likely to produce practical results quicker.

AP One of the hopes of our research is that what will come out of it is a very strong policy-driven recommendation for something like that to be set up. From here we could move to assets. Is art still an alternative asset class?

AW It was always an asset class.

KM The financial world looks upon it as a method of spreading its risk
financially and in the world of increased threats of deflation, inflation etc.,
if you don't spread your risk, you are deemed a bad manager of funds.

AP I've also read analyses that have suggested that, from about the 2000s
onwards, there was a great investment in art as an alternative asset class
that actually didn't really prove its worth. It was maybe alternative in terms
of spreading the risk but it wasn't alternative in terms of increased profit.

KM And why was that? Perhaps because some of the people who were doing
it hadn't got a clue what the art was about and they themselves sought advice
from people who were commission/fee/turnover driven.

AP I'm thinking specifically about start-ups like the Mei Moses Fine Art Index.

KM Purchasing art for investment purposes is not about living off commission
by way of trading. It is about doing what value investment is about, which is
getting it, holding it, watching it … waiting. That's why I go back to the premise
that if you really want to encourage a proper collection of art by individuals, you
should incentivise the activity in a way which means that, if you don't sell it in
under say five years, you get a better tax break than if you do, and in so doing one
might diminish the habit of 'flipping'.

AW You just go to auction. You look at the auction results.

AP How does Cabinet deal with and in this environment?

AW We've been absolutely concerned with managing not just the careers
of artists but the way information is conveyed, and the way we behave with
other dealers, the way they need to deal with work. So, yes, there's definitely
an element of control but we knew by the mid-'90s that some of what we
did, not all of it, would actually be long-lasting, would have a significant
effect not only on the marketplace but on the cultural reading in the future.

What we've written, what work we've had in the gallery, what text we've
commissioned and published, the way we behave in the gallery with collectors
or artists or members of the public, is absolutely crucial to the gallery's standing
and reputation.

AP Diametrically opposed to the art funds just described but somehow always relating to them.

KM Totally. But I think what you've also got to take into account is the commercial reality of how things change as time goes by. Large participating financial organisations, be they galleries, financial institutions or investors, who merely purchase art as an opportunity to exploit their financial position, will inevitably and ultimately have an adverse effect on that in which they participate.

AP Raze ...

AW Asset strip ...

KM Yes, exactly. In the nineteenth century Britain used to send from Newcastle to Australia what I think was called 'lace', i.e. cast iron railings that were used as ballast on ships. From Australia we used to take back whatever we could get: wool, gold, coal. I have a similar feeling of imbalance about today's arrangements referred to above.

I remember when I first left college: one was expected to serve out one's time, and then maybe someone would give you an exhibition a bit further down the line. Damien [Hirst] came up with the idea of putting on an artist-led exhibition called *Freeze*, back in 1988, the year that I left college. At the beginning, we imagined that we could do it for ourselves. We could circumnavigate the commercial gallery, we could represent ourselves, sell our own work and work for ourselves, but that didn't last very long.

Michael Landy, The Economy of Art, November 2009

It's interesting that art has retained its value at a time where other economies are collapsing. That means that art has another kind of value. The buzz in galleries in recent years hasn't been about the great contribution that this or that painter was making to the way everyone thinks about the world; the thing that was interesting to everyone was how much the paintings were selling for.

Susan Hiller, The Economy of Art, November 2009

I think we need artists because only artists can get us out of the recession. John Maynard Keynes said the same: that's why he set up the Arts Council. He said that you don't actually live [with] what the artist has done until long after: that's when you realise the virtues. Invest in it now, because if you look back, every great advance in civilisation is shaped by artists.

Alan Freeman, The Economy of Art, November 2009

If I had the power today I should surely set out to endow our capital cities with all the appurtenances of art and civilization on the highest standards of which the citizens of each were individually capable, convinced that what I could create, I could afford – and believing that the money thus spent would not only be better than any dole, but would make unnecessary any dole.

John Maynard Keynes, 'National self-sufficiency', *The Yale Review*, vol. 22, no. 4 (June 1933), pp. 755–69

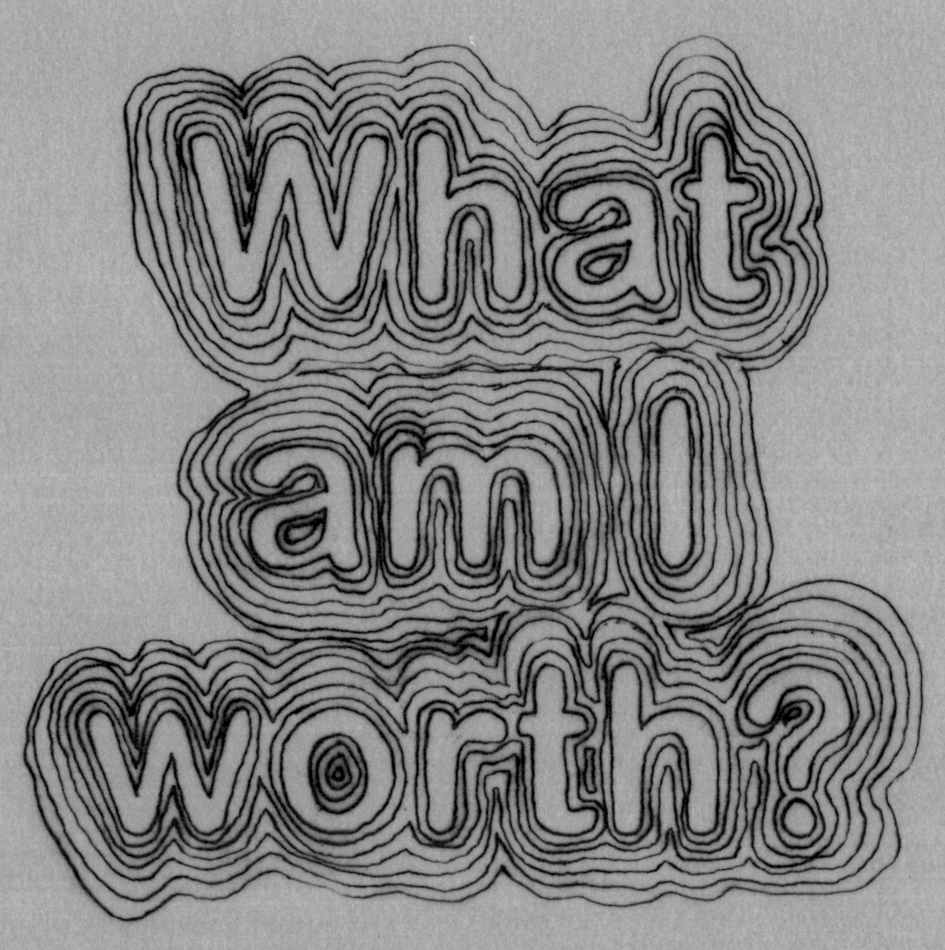
What
am I
worth?

What
am I
worth?

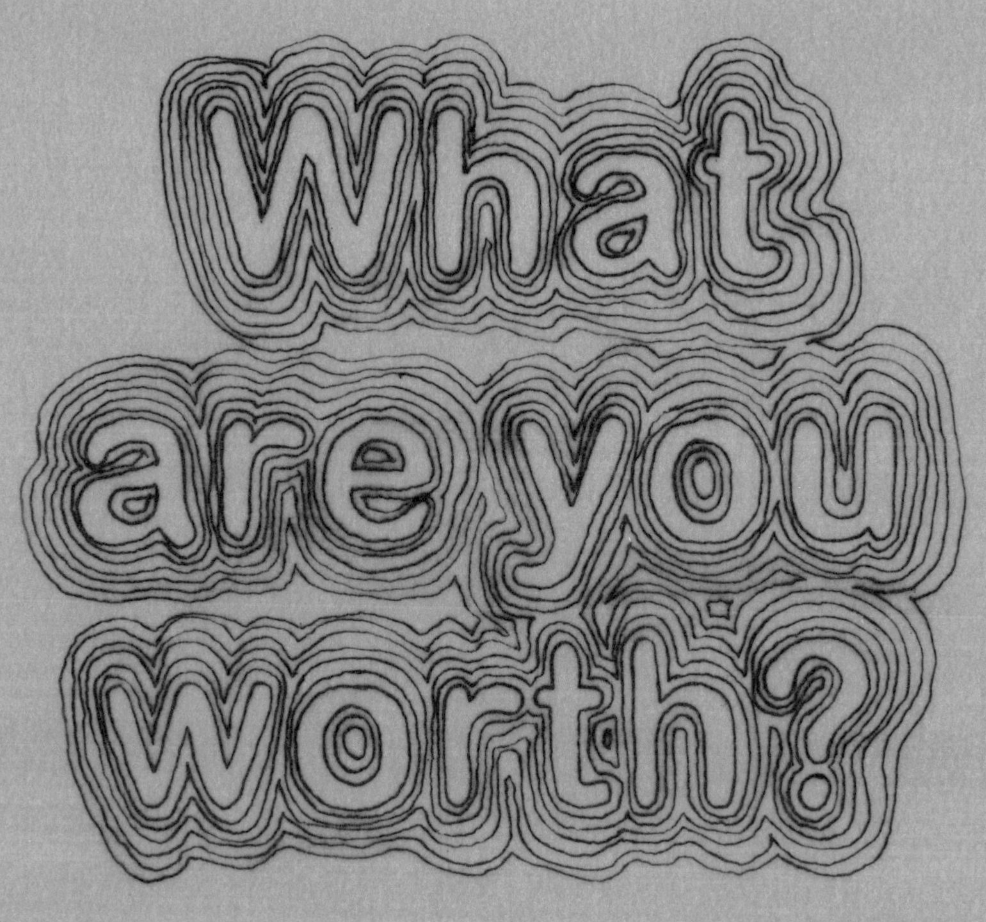

What
are you
worth?

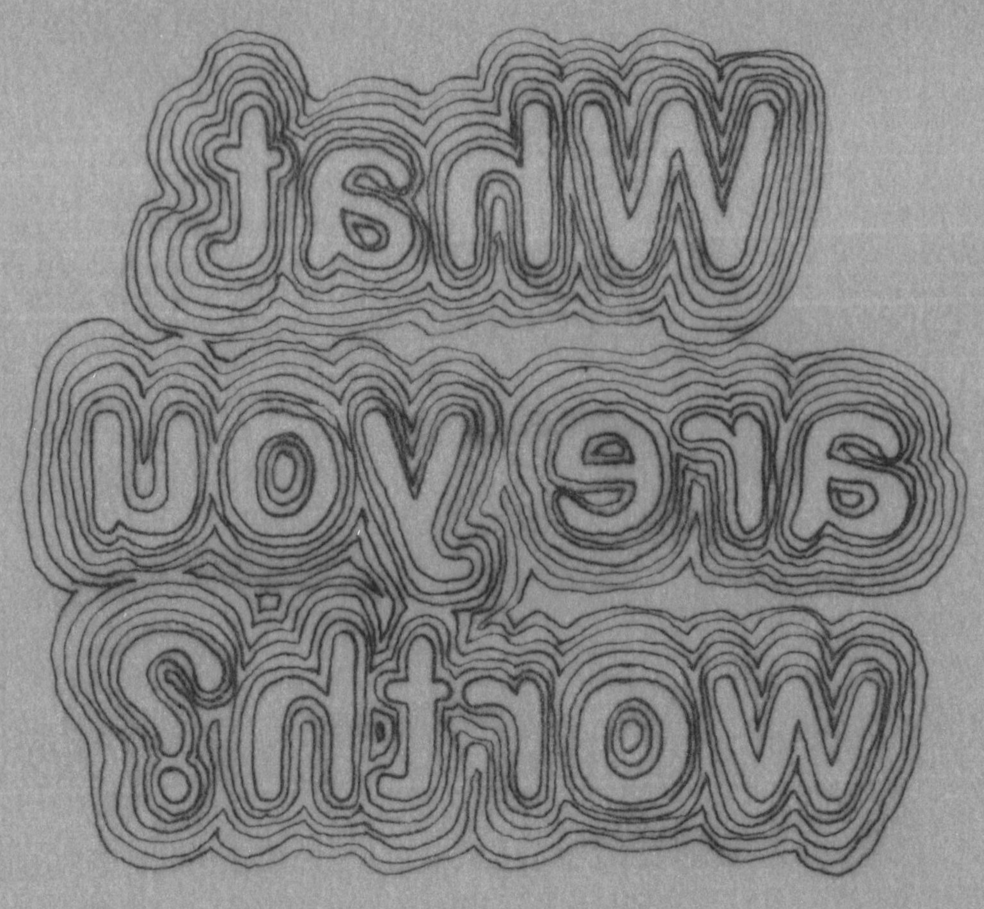

What
are you
worth?

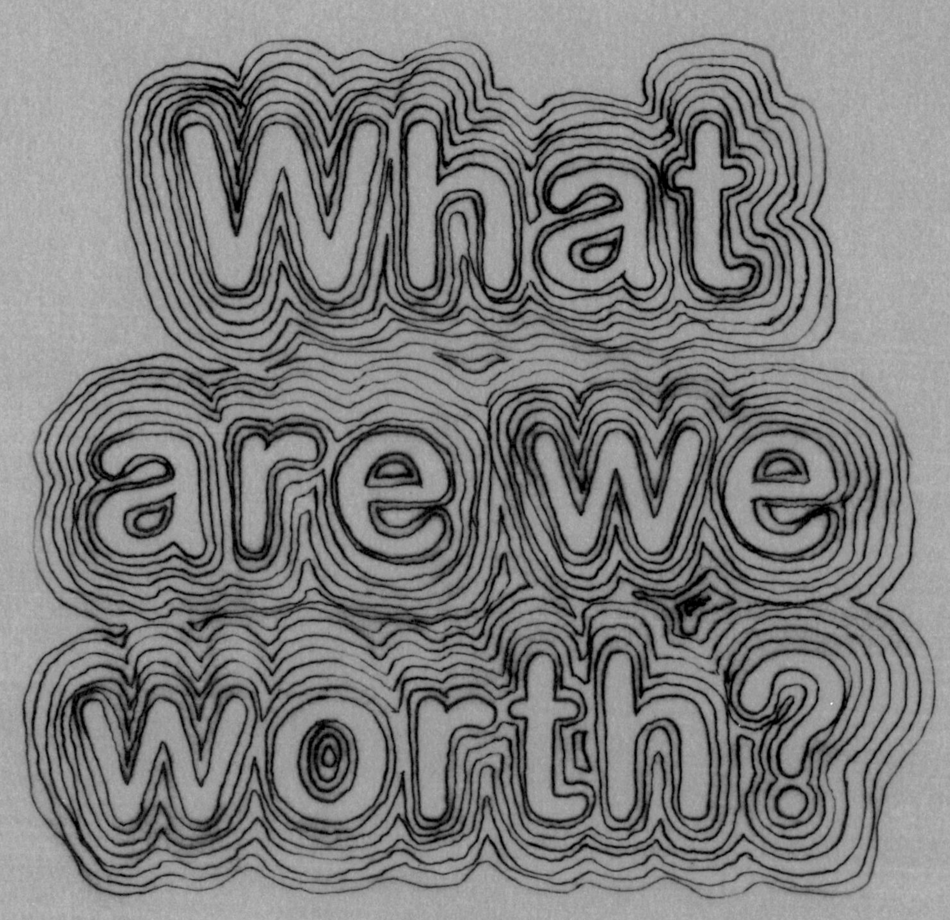
What
are we
worth?

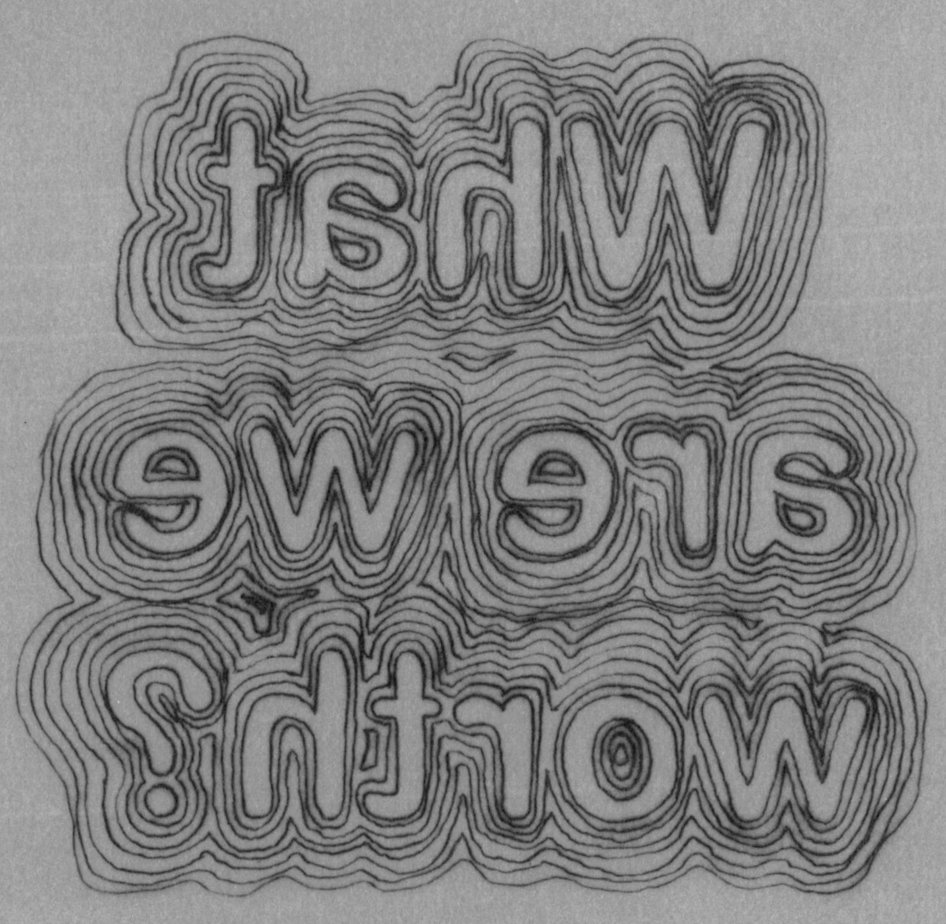

What
are we
worth?

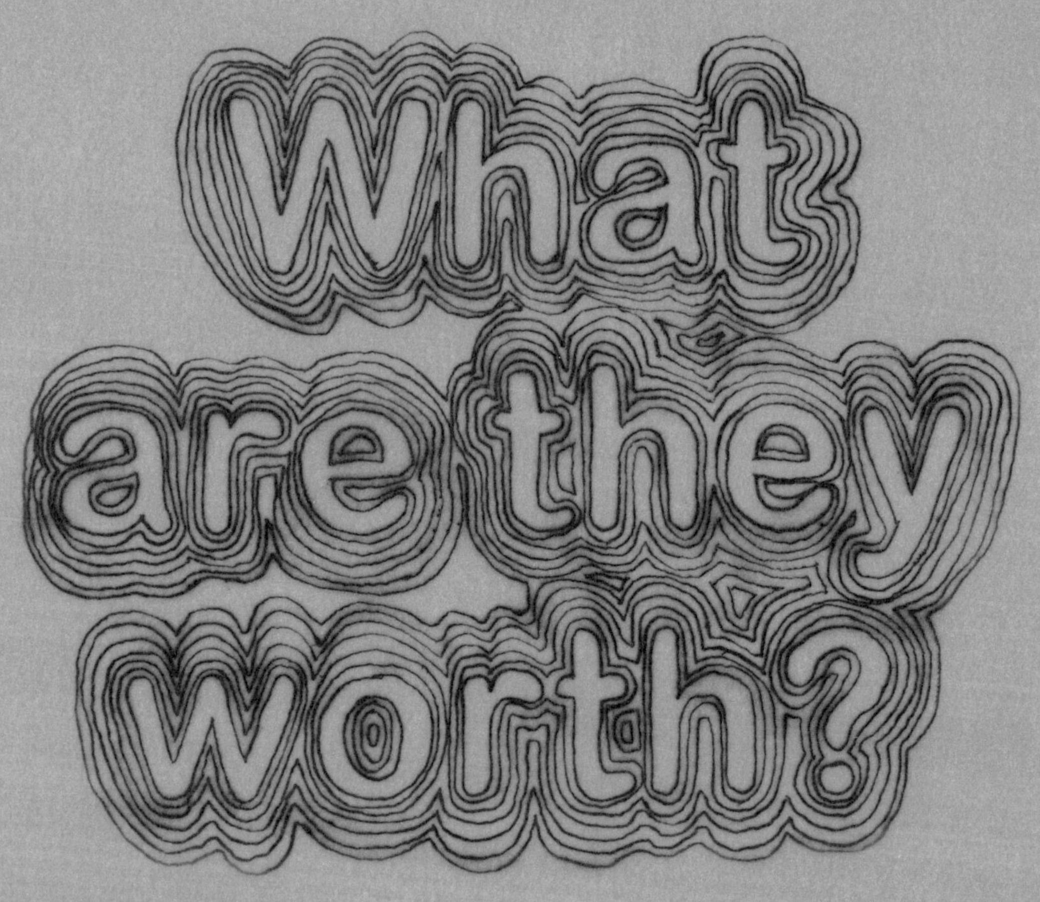

What
are they
worth?

What
are they
worth?

What am I worth?
Artistic intervention by Sonia Boyce, 2014

Lynda Morris

Genuine?

A casual comment made by a foreign curator at a conference in Birmingham suggested it may take many decades for Britain to recover from the Goldsmiths' young British artists (yBas). I have been thinking about this ever since and I have to go back over four decades to recover the story.

In my experience, 1968 was the year the international contemporary art world came into focus, against the backdrop of the escalation of the war in Vietnam and the fear of nuclear war against the USSR across a divided Germany. It was also the start of what is euphemistically called 'The Troubles' in Northern Ireland. After 12 years of war in Iraq and Afghanistan, we should be wondering why our artists have shown no comparable response in the last decade. The internationalism of the artists and dealers in the late 1960s and early 1970s was in response to mass protests by ordinary people against the financial, military, industrial and political interests that dominated capitalist countries. Since 1968, and particularly since 1989, the combined financial might of the military, industrial and political interests of the West and the East appears to have silenced the humanist values of artists.

The history of what I have lived through begins not only with the disasters inflicted on the people of Europe and Asia during the Second World War but also with the people's rebellion in 1968. The city of Hue was held by the Viet Cong against the US army's Tet Offensive in January 1968. US troops were increased by 10,000 and a US bombing assault on Hue resulted in massive destruction. In March there was a massacre of women and children in My Lai. It became the subject of an Art Workers' Coalition poster and demonstration in front of Pablo Picasso's *Guernica* (1937) at the MoMA in New York. Carl Andre and Robert Smithson were among the artists photographed holding the poster, which read:

Q. And Babies?
A. And Babies.

In March there was also violent street fighting in Rome with hundreds of people injured. The police closed the university for 12 days. In London, 10,000 demonstrators marched on the US Embassy in Grosvenor Square. Hundreds of people were injured by the 1,000 police on guard under the shadow of the concrete eagle. Marcel Broodthaers made the first exhibition in Brussels of his *Museum of Modern Art: Department of Eagles*.

On 4 April Martin Luther King Jr was assassinated in Memphis, Tennessee. From 4 to 8 April, 181 US cities were in flames including Washington and Chicago. In total, 43 people were killed, 2,135 people were wounded and 13,428 arrested; 20,000 federal troops and 40,000 national guards were deployed. Black GIs in Vietnam made up 14.9% of the troops, but there were only 11% of black people in the US population. Also in April, firebombs went off in two Frankfurt department stores. Andreas Baader, Gudrun Ensslin, Thorwald Proll and Horst Sohnlein, four members of the Baader-Meinhof group, were arrested, tried and sentenced to three years in prison. On 11 April, an assassination attempt on Rudi Dutschke, leader of the Marxist Socialist Students League in Berlin, led to street battles in the divided city.

On 3 May, 40,000 students were locked out of the Sorbonne in Paris. More than 10,000 students fought running battles and built barricades on the Left Bank fighting against the police, the *Garde Mobile* and the CRS riot police. Train stations and airports were closed and telephones cut off. A General Strike was called on 14 May. President de Gaulle fled to Bonn, Germany. In the UK, the six-week occupation of Hornsey College of Art started on 28 May. Croydon and Guildford Schools of Art were also occupied.

Bobby Kennedy was assassinated in Los Angeles on 5 June; on 7 June over one million people protested on the streets of Paris. Demonstrators at the Venice Biennale issued a manifesto:

The Biennale ... is one of those moments when the mechanics of the authorities' oppression is concretised. It is true that the product of art in the capitalist society, by virtue of being 'expensive toys for intellectuals of the ruling classes', is a phenomenon that concerns but a limited number of people. But the cultural modes that are created by the organisation of capitalist culture put their mark on the whole of society.

In Venice the Argentine artist David Lamelas installed a bureau titled *The Office of Information about the Vietnam War at Three Levels: The Visual Image, Text and Audio (1968)*. Belgrade University was occupied by students. *Documenta 4* opened to protests between the organisers and the Social Democratic Students Organisation, the latter complaining there were only two politically committed artists out of 117 exhibitors: Ed Kienholz and Oyvind Fahlstrom. Dutch artists occupied the Rembrandt Night Watch Hall Rijksmuseum, Amsterdam. The Poor People's March on Washington took place on 24 June.

It was on 3 August that Nigeria's Biafran famine started to appear in the media. Soviet, East German, Polish, Hungarian and Bulgarian troops moved into Czechoslovakia on 20 August ending the 'Prague Awakening' of leader Alexander Dubcek. Senator Eugene McCarthy campaigned for the US presidency with Picasso's *Dove of Peace*, first used in 1949. At the Chicago Democratic Convention on 29 August, McCarthy and George McGovern were defeated by Hubert Humphrey. The French writer Jean Genet, the US poet Allen

Ginsberg and US writer William Burroughs were photographed together at the Convention. On the streets, 10,000 people demonstrated and were attacked by 5,000 National Guards and 12,000 police on the orders of Mayor Daley; 250 people were injured. Norman Mailer wrote *Miami and the Siege of Chicago* in a month. An exhibition at Richard L. Feigen & Co. included the Abstract Expressionist Barnett Newman's *Mayor Daley's Lace Curtain*, a painted grid of barbed wire splattered with red paint representing blood.

On 5 October the first major Republican demonstration in Londonderry started 'The Troubles' in Northern Ireland. There were riots at the Mexico Olympics on 12 October, where Tommie Smith and John Carlos gave the Black Power salute from the medals podium. Mrs Nguyen Thi Binh, a North Vietnamese leader, arrived for peace negotiations in Paris on 4 November. On 5 November Republican Richard Nixon won the US election and Russian tanks entered Prague.

Moral outrage was widely felt by artists and their dealers. In the USA, South America, West Germany, France, Italy, Britain and Eastern Europe, dissident artists began to work together internationally to develop a new art world. They were not revolutionaries but they were reformers. During the late 1960s and early 1970s there was a reformation of the idea that contemporary art was about riches rather than humanity.

By the early 1970s it is estimated that 354,112 US GIs had gone AWOL and an estimated 30% of the GIs in Vietnam had developed a heroin habit, making a large contribution to the withdrawal of the US from Vietnam. Canada, South America, Europe and London were havens for US draft dodgers. National Service in Britain ended in 1960, while the draft in the US continued until the close of the Vietnam War in 1973. There has been little discussion in Britain and the USA about the fact that the end of National Service and the draft meant there was no longer 'a people's army' in the Western democracies. I had never made an association between the British army's deployment in Northern Ireland on 14 August 1969 and the end of National Service. Then our army shot dead 13 protesters in Belfast on 30 January 1972, 'Bloody Sunday'. I could not believe it. Fernand Spillemaeckers, the founder of the MTL Gallery in Brussels, showed work by Broodthaers, Daniel Buren, Art & Language, Carl Andre, Lawrence Weiner and Andre Cadere. He talked to me in 1974 about the relationship between Britain's professional army and 'The Troubles':

You only need to look at European History to know what happens when you no longer have a People's Army, you have a Mercenary Army, and it is no longer controlled by the will of the people. That is why your army is still in Northern Ireland.

I thought of this conversation often over the years. The British army stayed in Northern Ireland for 38 years until 31 July 2007. The wars in Iraq and Afghanistan from 2001 to 2014 cost the British people £65 billion on top of the normal defence budget (£38 to £47 billion a year) and 782 armed forces personnel were killed in the two wars. Would this have happened if we had still had National Service, conscription, a 'people's army' representing a wide cross-section of public opinion, rather than a 'professional army'?

When the dealer Konrad Fischer came to Norwich in 1993 to select the third annual *EAST International* exhibition, we talked about the 1970s, when we drank and danced with Gilbert & George, and I asked him how he had been able to do what he did? Meaning, how did he, a young artist, bring together US, British and European artists into a new movement, Conceptual Art? In subsequent years I brought to Norwich as selectors for *EAST International* other figures of that first generation with whom I shared this history: the dealers Nicholas Logsdail, Jack Wendler, Michel Durand-Dessert and Marian Goodman, and the artists Jan Dibbets, Giuseppe Penone, Richard Long, Weiner, and Art & Language. My conversations with all of them touched on the loss of dissident voices in the work of artists today.

I respected the innovative primary art dealers of the late 1960s as being the real intelligence behind Conceptual Art, but they have largely been written out of history. These dealers understood the connections between artists in different countries; they gave artists their first international exhibitions, networked them and included them in mixed-nationality exhibitions: Konrad Fischer (Düsseldorf), Anny De Decker (Wide White Space, Antwerp), Adriaan van Ravesteijn (Art and Project, Amsterdam), Nigel Greenwood and Nicholas Logsdail (London), Gian Enzo Sperone (Turin), Yvon Lambert and Ileana Sonnabend (Paris), Paul Maenz (Cologne) and Fernand Spillemaeckers (MTL, Brussels).

In 1995-96 I undertook 14 hours of interviews with Peter Townsend on his editing of *Studio International* from 1965 to 1975. Townsend came from a Quaker background and went to China in 1940 as an ambulance driver. He stayed there during the Communist Revolution, only returning to Britain around 1953. In 1995 Townsend debated with Seth Siegelaub, Terry Atkinson and myself in Norwich. The title of the debate – 'The Refurbishment of Conceptualism' – was suggested by Atkinson and was a reference to the refurbishment of the Reagan White House. Central to the discussions was the then contemporary failure of artists to challenge the dominance of the monetary value of art over human values: riches rather than humanity. Even when radical artists from the 1960s and 1970s are given major retrospectives, the initial political influences on their art are concealed. Their experience with the draft or National Service is hardly ever recorded.

I consider Conceptual Art to have been a true avant-garde between 1967 and 1973. My definition of avant-garde is influenced by Donald Drew Egbert's *Social Radicalism and the Arts, Western Europe: a Cultural History from the French Revolution to 1968* (1970). Egbert shows that avant-garde movements are not stylistic; the connection between them is that they are formed during, or in the aftermath of, wars. Nowhere was this period of Conceptual Art felt more intensely than in the divided Germany and in the US, where artists knew that the Vietnam War and conflicts in Cambodia and Laos were continuations of the US Second World War and the Korean War engagement with the Asian countries bordering the Pacific Ocean.

Political geography is one way to look at the list of exhibitions Fischer prepared for his interview with Georg Jappe. He defined his job as repairing the damage of war:

To get artists over here, and to bring them into contact with those who live here. When I was an artist everything was so far away; Warhol, Lichtenstein and all those were unattainable great men. But when you know them, you can have a beer with them and get rid of your inferiority complex … Palermo and Richter, for example, two of the German artists who have exhibited with me, have now been to New York, and they felt at home there because they had already met artists like Andre and LeWitt over here.[1]

The first mixed-nationality international exhibition of Conceptual Art in Europe was *Prospect 68: Internationale Vorschau auf die Kunst in den Galerien der Avantgarde* (*Prospect 68: International Preview of the Art in the Galleries of the Avant-garde*) at Düsseldorf Kunsthalle, 20–29 September 1968, organised by Konrad Fischer and Hans Strelow.

It took place a month after the close of *Documenta 4* in Kassel and was in great contrast to that exhibition, which included only five artists connected with the emerging Conceptual network: Carl Andre, Donald Judd, Robert Morris, Bruce Nauman and Sol LeWitt, who were then all seen as US Minimalist sculptors. *Documenta* was founded in 1955 in Kassel, only ten miles from the 'Iron Curtain'.

Annie de Decker and Bernd Lohaus of Wide White Space, Antwerp, hired two ground-floor reception rooms of the Parkhaus Hotel in Kassel for the first week of *Documenta 4*. They showed artists from their gallery, including Broodthaers, Panamarenko, Joseph Beuys, Christo and Piero Manzoni. Lohaus had studied at the Düsseldorf Kunstakademie and he knew the Capitalist Realists: Gerhard Richter, Sigmar Polke and Konrad (Leug) Fisher. Richter and Polke were both émigrés from the German Democratic Republic (DDR). Fischer's mother came from a Mennonite, pacifist family.

In October 1967 Fischer opened his space in Düsseldorf between the Kunsthalle and the Kunstakademie. He rented a tunnel between two buildings and fitted the front and back with glass doors so the exhibitions could be seen even when the space was closed. He was working as a teacher and he opened for just a few hours in the afternoon. He had the idea that if he sent artists a plane ticket and let them stay in his flat in Düsseldorf, and had their work made locally, there would be no expensive international transport costs involved.

It was less than a year later that Fischer worked with Strelow to develop *Prospect 68*. They invited 16 galleries from eight countries, chosen by an independent committee, including Alan Bowness from London. The galleries selected the artists they wanted to show and they paid all their own costs, transport and artists expenses because *Prospect 68* offered them access to the *Kunstmarkt* collectors, without the fees. The galleries included: Robert Fraser, Kasmin and Axiom (Nigel Greenwood), Lambert, Sonnabend, Dwan, Sperone and Wide White Space. The artists included: Giovanni Anselmo, Beuys, Boetti, Broodthaers, Christo, Walter de Maria, David Lamelas, John Latham, Mario Merz, Morris, Nauman, Blinky Palermo and Panamarenko. The emphasis was on cities, not on national identities. The first Cologne *Kunstmarkt*, in 1967, had been open only to German galleries.

Included in *Prospect 68* by Ileana Sonnabend was Mario Merz's *Giap's Igloo* (1968), which Merz made especially for the exhibition. The neon lettering quotes the North Vietnamese General Võ Nguyên Giáp: 'Se il nemico si concentra perde terreno se il nemico si disperde perde forza' (If the enemy masses his forces, he loses ground. If he scatters, he loses force). Merz talked to me in 1975 about his experiences carrying messages for the Communist Resistance in Italy in the late stages of the Second World War. Documentation of the exhibition shows clearly that *Prospect 68* brought together work that would dominate the following decades. Curator and art historian Harald Szeemann was at the opening. Nigel Greenwood, of Axiom and the Courtauld Institute, was so excited by the exhibition that he came back to London and encouraged art historian Charles Harrison to go. A month after *Prospect 68*, there are photographs of Fischer and Richard Long at the opening of *Arte Povera + Azioni Povere* at the Arsenale in Amalfi.

Prospect 68 was about artists with new ideas focused by the political events of the year. The ideas came from cities devastated by the Second World War. Many of the original generation of dealers were artists themselves and they held an innate respect for the artists with whom they chose to work. They had no time for theory; the catalogue was a cheap newspaper. The now famous, younger artists who emerged from Düsseldorf in the 1970s and 1980s talked to me about Fischer's 'moral authority'.

Britain does not understand the European culture of cities because there is only one city that matters in Britain – London. However, London galleries were only secondary partners to the European galleries. Those galleries were often in small European cities with art academies, where the dealers were able to focus clearly on promoting the new Conceptual Art. When he selected *EAST* in 1994, Jan Dibbets talked about the artists based in small provincial cities: Richard Long in Bristol, Art & Language in Coventry, Bernd and Hilla Becher and Richter in Düsseldorf, Merz in Turin, Broodthaers in Brussels and himself in Amsterdam. There is also a tendency for institutions in Britain to make everything British. *The New Art* show 1972 included only British artists, the Turner Prize is all about British artists, then we have the *The British Art Show* and the yBa movement with the capital B for young *British* artists.

Greenwood's involvement with *Prospect 68* led him to start his own gallery in Glebe Place, Chelsea, in 1970, showing Gilbert & George's *Singing Sculpture* (1969). Nicholas Logsdail, an ex-Slade theatre design student, started the Lisson Gallery in the mid-1960s, organised the *Wall Show* in December 1970, and then went on to make exhibitions with LeWitt, Judd and Andre in 1971. The Situation Gallery, off Brook Street, London, showed work by Bruce McLean, Hamish Fulton and Gilbert & George. In late December 1971, the US émigré Jack Wendler opened a gallery in North Gower Street, London, with work by US and European artists including Weiner, Robert Barry, Douglas Huebler, John Baldessari, Dibbets, Buren and Broodthaers.

It seems unfair that credit is still not paid to the dealers who pulled the international threads together, not only for the artists, but also for the curators, critics, theorists and bureaucrats who followed in their wake. I often wonder whether the lack of truth about the importance of the intellectual role of the first generation of dealers in the late 1960s and early 1970s may have distorted our understanding of the role of those dealers, and that may have led us to overestimate the role of curators, critics and the secondary dealers who followed in their wake? This is certainly true of my experience of working at the Institute of Contemporary Arts (ICA) during the installation of *When Attitudes Become Form* in August 1969. Konrad Fischer was there all day everyday, working out of the gallery office. Charles Harrison was assistant editor at *Studio International* and teaching with Anthony Caro at St Martins, and he spent the installation period juggling all three roles. Harald Szeemann arrived in London just in time to make the opening speech.

Because of the diverse cities in most European countries, the idea of a moral, political and dissident contemporary art has been able to survive, to some extent. That held true in Britain for most of the 1970s with exhibitions curated by Barry

Barker at the ICA, Michael Crompton and Anne Seymour at the Tate Gallery and
the international shows in the programme of Nicholas Serota and Sandy Nairne
at the Museum of Modern Art (MOMA) in Oxford. In August 1972 Seymour,
an Assistant Keeper at the Tate Gallery, organised the first survey show of recent
British Art at the Hayward Gallery. *The New Art* show was devoted to British artists
who were part of the international network of Conceptual Art and opened two
months after *Documenta 5*. However provincial the exhibition appeared, Seymour
emerged as a respected contact at the Tate Gallery, which then began to purchase
international Conceptual Art. The Arts Council officer who assisted Seymour
was a Cambridge and Courtauld graduate, Nicholas Serota. Serota travelled
to Germany that autumn with Michael Craig-Martin, who up until then had
not been considered a Conceptual Artist and was therefore a surprise inclusion
in Seymour's exhibition. Serota visited *Documenta 5*, Konrad Fischer's space
in Düsseldorf and the Cologne *Kunstmart*. I was on the same flight to Cologne,
as I was going to observe Beuys's teaching in Düsseldorf for my RCA thesis.

In 1973 Serota was appointed director of MOMA in Oxford following the
pioneering programme of Peter Ibsen. Serota helped me to write an account
of MOMA Oxford for *Studio International* in 1975.[2] In three years, despite a
major financial depression caused by the devaluation of the pound, Serota's
Arts Council of Great Britain (ACGB) funding tripled from £10,000 to £30,000.
In 1976 he was appointed director of the Whitechapel Gallery. The programme
at Oxford, and initially at the Whitechapel, followed the artists associated with
the international network in Europe including: Andre, LeWitt, Hanne Darboven,
Dibbets, Robert Ryman, Ulrich Rüchriem, Richter, the Bechers, Long, Fulton
and Gilbert & George.

On 16 February 1976 the *Daily Mirror* published a front-page article, 'What
a Load of Rubbish', about the Tate Gallery's purchase of Carl Andre's 'Bricks'
from the John Weber Gallery in 1972. Four years later, in July 1976, the painter
R.B. Kitaj organised *The Human Clay* at the Hayward Gallery, an ACGB touring
exhibition. It gathered together the figurative painters in London and named
them the 'School of London'. Many of the key figures of the School were from
émigré families. The exhibition was a great success. Kitaj and David Hockney
mounted a campaign for a return to Life Drawing as the basis of art education.
They attracted a younger generation of critics, including Timothy Hyman and
Peter Fuller. They also supported the exhibition I organised with Andrew Brighton
for the Midland Group, Nottingham, *Towards Another Picture* (1977), which led
to the conference titled *The State of British Art: A Debate* at the ICA in 1978.

A number of German galleries had dared to set their sights on New York
30 years after the Second World War. Reinhardt Onnasch started the move

with a Richter exhibition, organised by Fischer, in September 1973. Heiner Friedrich followed and then Sperone Westwater Fischer (the latter was the name of the gallery Fischer opened with Angela Westwater. It survives today as Sperone Westwater). Angela Westwater was Andre's girlfriend and the business editor of *Artforum*. Michael Werner, the owner of a small Cologne gallery, visited a handful of artists in East Germany and returned to the West with their canvases in the boot of his car. By the late 1970s his German artists were beginning to compete with Fischer's American, European and British Conceptual Artists in international networks.

Serota at the Whitechapel led the way in Britain showing work by Markus Lüpertz in 1979 and by Georg Baselitz in 1980. He laid down the art historical reference with Max Beckmann's *Triptychs* in November 1980 and with work by Philip Guston in 1982.

May 1979 saw the massacre of the spirit of 1968, with the election of Margaret Thatcher as Prime Minister. The Conservative government was helped to win the election by Saatchi & Saatchi's advertising campaign, 'Labour Isn't Working'. In the first three years of Thatcher's government, two million UK jobs were lost. By April 1982 we were at war with Argentina over the Falkland Islands. In March 1984 the closure of 20 pits was announced; the miners' strike began, and lasted until March 1985.

Also in 1979, Anne Seymour resigned from the Tate Gallery and married Anthony d'Offay, a dealer who was successful at selling the estates of Bloomsbury artists, which enabled him to take on Lucian Freud and others. A second d'Offay Gallery was opened in 1980, specialising in the international avant-garde. The couple's first exhibition was of the work of Lawrence Weiner, arranged for them by Konrad Fischer.

London galleries showing Conceptual Art survived on sales to British public collections. London dealers had long dreamed of a really major collector emerging in Britain, and in late 1979 and early 1980 their dream came true in the form of Charles and Doris Saatchi. They began buying not just one or two new paintings here and there but whole exhibitions. The d'Offay Gallery picked up a lot of the Saatchi patronage. Bruce McLean sold his entire 1982 exhibition in the first week of his show with d'Offay. In the second week I saw him delivering more paintings. Saatchi's support also helped Logsdail to launch the Lisson, and the artists Richard Deacon, Bill Woodrow, Tony Cragg and Anish Kapoor, who had been taken on by the Lisson after Weiner, Long and Andre moved to the d'Offay Gallery.

In 1980 Norman Rosenthal persuaded the Royal Academy of Arts, London, to hold a painting exhibition. He argued from the position of Hockney and Kitaj that artists were returning to painting. *A New Spirit in Painting* (1981) was organised by Rosenthal, Christo Joachimides and Serota. Picasso, Balthus, Francis Bacon, Freud, Frank Auerbach, Kitaj and Hockney were a backdrop to German Neo-Expressionists and US painters from Guston to Julian Schnabel. Charles and Doris Saatchi appeared in the list of acknowledgements at the front of the catalogue. The exhibition was financed by grants from the Arts Council, the West German government, the West Berlin senate and 'two anonymous private donations'. If these donations came from people with a financial involvement in *The New Art* at the Hayward Gallery, it was an intelligent investment, because the RA exhibition did a great deal to encourage museum purchases and raised the value of the work exhibited.

Tracing the term 'The New Art' reveals the increasing influence on public sector institutions in London of a small number of curators. Some of those curators were in contact with industrialists, bankers and property developers who were all seeking to make London the 'great European financial capital'. They in turn were served by a new generation of secondary dealers who, unlike the first generation of Conceptual Art dealers, were more concerned with money than they were with moral authority.

When discussing public funding of the arts in Britain, it is useful to distinguish between two strands: firstly, grants to public sector galleries through Arts Council England (ACE) (previously ACGB); and, secondly, purchase grants for public collections. The latter can be seen as the public funding of private dealer galleries, which would expect to receive 50% of the purchase price. Based in London are: Tate's national and international collections of contemporary art; Arts Council Collection; British Council Collection; Contemporary Arts Society; The Art Fund (formerly the National Art Collections Fund); Government Art Collection; Victoria and Albert Museum; and British Museum. This is a major reason why dealer galleries are all clustered in London. Germany, Italy and France (since the development of French Regional Contemporary Art Funds (FRAC)) are all based on traditional city states, and their public funding and collecting structures are devolved.

Public collections of contemporary art in Britain keep confidential the price they pay for art, arguing that this enables the dealer to give them special discounts. My knowledge of dealers suggests the opposite. The dealers use the public collections to establish prices, and those prices are then discounted for private collectors. However, price confidentiality makes it difficult to check the facts.

In June 1982 the Tate Gallery announced the formation of the 'Patrons of New Art'. The inaugural development was Julian Schnabel's first museum exhibition, which opened at the Tate on 30 June. Schnabel's meteoric rise had started two years earlier. Mary Boon and Leo Castelli promoted him as New York's answer to the new German and Italian artists. A show for Schnabel at the Tate must have been beyond their dreams. It had taken Castelli almost a decade to achieve a Tate retrospective for Andy Warhol, and two decades for Robert Rauschenberg. With the exception of one recent painting purchased by the Tate for its collection, nine of the remaining ten paintings by Schnabel in the exhibition came from the 'Collection of Charles and Doris Saatchi'. Some time in 1982, Serota appointed Charles Saatchi a trustee of the Whitechapel and Saatchi & Saatchi appeared on the list of financial benefactors of the gallery.

In early 1982 Saatchi & Saatchi took over Compton Communications in New York. Charles Saatchi's role in supporting the one-man exhibition at the Tate for Schnabel was a brilliant stroke that ensured him a warm welcome by the top drawer of American society, through the social role of museums among the rich, powerful and corporate in the USA.

In November 1982, a d'Offay Gallery press release was pleased to commend the developing relationship between New Art in New York and the Tate Gallery:

This summer we showed 'Walking the Dog', one of David Salle's recent pictures … We found our visitors fascinated, although most of them had never seen Salle's work before. The Tate Gallery, already well informed, bought the painting.

The year 1983 at the Whitechapel began with a Francesco Clemente exhibition, *The Fourteen Stations of the Cross*, on 7 January. The d'Offay Gallery also opened a Clemente show on the same evening and a coach was laid on to take art lovers between the two openings. The Clemente paintings at the Whitechapel had been made in New York in the preceding two months, as Mark Francis's interview with the artist for the Whitechapel exhibition leaflet recorded, but they were shown at the Whitechapel 'Courtesy of the Collection of Charles and Doris Saatchi'. By May 1984 Fritz Mondale, the US Democratic Party candidate, had announced the appointment of Saatchi & Saatchi as the party's advertising agents for the forthcoming elections.

In January 1984 an exhibition of work by Hans Haacke, the New York-based German artist, was due to open at the Tate Gallery. Haacke specialised in documentary exposures of the political implications of the business interests of the wealthy people involved with the museums and galleries where he was invited to show. He had traced links between the overthrow of President Salvador Allende in Chile and the board of the Solomon R. Guggenheim Museum, and for *Manet-PROJEKT '74* he traced the Jewish owner in the 1930s of Édouard Manet's *Bunch of Asparagus* (1880) in the collection of the Wallraf-Richartz

Museum, Cologne. Both these exhibitions were cancelled. *Private Eye* revealed Haacke was researching Saatchi & Saatchi. The Tate decided not to cancel Haacke's exhibition but the catalogue was pulped. In Haacke's 1983–84 painting of Margaret Thatcher, the bookcase behind her shows that Saatchi & Saatchi's clients included the South African Nationalist Party as well as the British Conservative Party.

Charles Saatchi resigned from the Committee of the Patrons of New Art in February 1984, although he remained a member. At the time Saatchi & Saatchi also held the advertising account for the Tate Gallery. In the same month, Saatchi resigned as a trustee of the Whitechapel Art Gallery. It is impossible to state that Saatchi resigned because of the Haacke exhibition but it is a coincidence. In a conversation with Haacke in *October: The First Decade 1976–86*, Douglas Crimp alleged another reason:

> ... the fact that Doris and Charles Saatchi bought works by Malcolm Morley, after Charles Saatchi learned in a Whitechapel Gallery trustees meeting that that the gallery planned to stage a Morley exhibition.[3]

On 6 November 1984, the day of Ronald Reagan's re-election as President of the United States, *Omnibus*, the BBC1 arts programme, announced the winner of the first Turner Prize of £10,000. The annual prize, donated by an anonymous 'Patron of New Art', was to be awarded to the person who:

> ... in the opinion of 'The New Art Jury', has made the greatest contribution to art in Britain in the previous twelve months.[4]

The jury consisted of: Alan Bowness, director of the Tate Gallery; the art dealer Felicity Waley-Cohen (née Samuel), daughter of Viscount Bearsted, the honorary president of the trustees of the Whitechapel Art Gallery; Nicholas Serota, director of the Whitechapel; Rudi Fuchs, director of the Van Abbe Museum in Eindhoven; and John McEwen, art critic member of the brewing family. The shortlist for the £10,000 award was: Malcolm Morley, Richard Deacon, Howard Hodgkin, Richard Long and Gilbert & George. Morley won and all the other artists won in subsequent years.

In 1985 the property developer Peter Palumbo, chairman of the trustees of the Whitechapel, was appointed chairman of the Tate trustees by Margaret Thatcher. Palumbo owned houses by Frank Lloyd Wright and Mies van der Rohe in the US and a Le Corbusier house in France. In a full-page newspaper interview shortly after his appointment, Palumbo criticised the conservative approach of the director of the Tate Gallery, Alan Bowness, and praised the radicalism of the director of the Whitechapel Gallery, Nicholas Serota. Palumbo subsequently resigned as chair of the Tate trustees and was replaced by the architect Richard Rogers. Serota was appointed director of the Tate Gallery in 1988.

In this period architects were promoted as important cultural figures, for example, Richard Rogers, Norman Foster, Max Gordon, Will Allsop and John Pulson. In 1986 the Labour MP Mark Fisher, spokesman on arts and media and then spokesman for the Department for National Heritage, and Richard Rogers organised an exhibition at the RA, *London As It Could Be*. Their book, *A New London* (1992), was, in retrospect, the blueprint for projects such as the Millenium Dome, Tate Modern and the 2012 London Olympics. The book tells us that, in 1991, 400 Local Authority houses were built in London and 800,000 people were homeless. It was the moment in late Thatcherism when the state no longer provided social housing and, instead, the national lottery, a new arm of the gambling industry, enabled museum directors and their trustees to start to plan Palaces of Culture.

In 1988 Margaret Thatcher forgave Peter Palumbo and appointed him chairman of the ACGB; he stayed in the unpaid job until 1994. He presided over the drafting of the rules for the allocation of an estimated £200 million a year national lottery funding for the 'good cause' of the arts. Palumbo's committee rejected the proposal put forward by the officers at ACGB, in cooperation with the artists' collectives ACME and SPACE, for a grand St Katherine's Dock-type regeneration of derelict industrial buildings for low-cost studios, housing and artist-led galleries throughout Britain.

Instead we were all taught the curious term 'subsidiarity', which meant lottery funding had to be spent on new projects. It could not be used to support activities the Arts Council was already funding. Everyone murmured approval not realising it meant that lottery funding would all be spent on high-end new galleries and museums in vast industrial conversions, which in turn would lead to urban regeneration, that is, very expensive urban property developments. Lottery funding for the 'good cause' of the arts was not allowed to benefit artists or programmes of their exhibitions, at least initially.

Palumbo was created a life peer by Thatcher in 1991, becoming Baron Palumbo of Walbrook, in the City of London. He was not the first property developer to take an interest in the visual arts; others include Alistair McAlpine, Janet de Botton, Jill Ritblat, and David and Max Gordon. Max Gordon designed the first Saatchi Gallery, and John Pulson married the art dealer and ex-wife of Nigel Greenwood, Hester van Royen. The gallery-museum-collector complex was firmly in charge of British art. The term 'international' lost the visionary meaning of the late 1960s. In the decade from 1974 to 1984, 'international' became synonymous with corporations, which became the most influential voices in the art world. Talking about success meant that corporate sponsorship and fundraising were the name of the game.

In the late 1980s the London art world appeared more regularly on the pages of *Vogue, Harper's, Tatler* and *World of Interiors* than it did in *Artforum*. Saatchi showed his *Sensation* collection at the RA in 1997, through Norman Rosenthal. Michael Craig-Martin was a trustee of the Tate Gallery for ten years from 1989 to 1999. That was the decade between the *Freeze* exhibition of the yBas and the preparations for the opening of Tate Modern in 2000.

The new trustees were art collectors, but their real qualification was their money. They replaced the art historians, the academics tarred in the period as Marxists, whose lifetime was devoted to the study and teaching of art. The Tate Annual Report in 2013 tells us that all four Tates are governed by a single board of trustees with 14 members. Three of the trustees are youngish artists and one is an art historian. The other ten are businessmen and women. A short time carrying out Google searches reveals their international corporate interests.

As the rock group *Wild Beasts* complained in the *Guardian* in February 2014:

It's the Damien Hirst effect: where does the chequebook end and the art begin?

1   *Studio International*, vol.181, February 1971, pp.68–71
2   'The Museum of Modern Art in Oxford 1965 to 1975', *Studio International*, vol.190, November/ December 1975
3   *October: The First Decade 1976-86* (Cambridge, MA: MIT Press, 1987), pp.175–200
4   Tate Gallery press release, quoted in 'Hot Art: The Turner Prize', *Radio Times*, 3 November 1984

Conceptual Engineer in Context

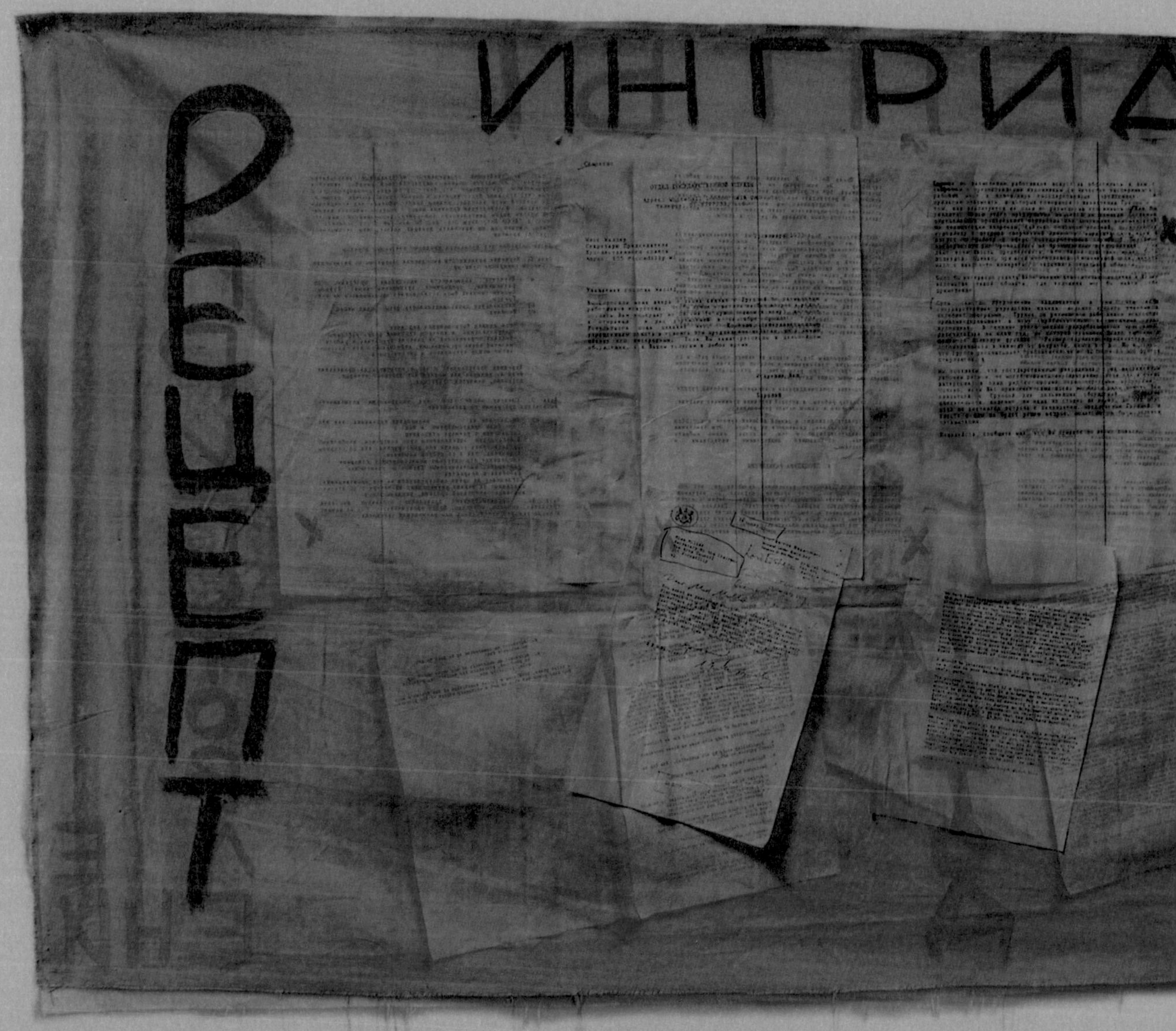

banner BANNER made for *Borscht* exhibition, St Petersburg (1993). Containing pages of APGs Civil Service Memorandum (1973) with Russian translations.
vision BANNER sent to *Antagonismes* exhibition at MACBA, Barcelona (2001) as a rolled up piece of un-stretched canvas.
product BANNER returned in a bespoke wooden shipping crate.

Conceptual Engineer in Context

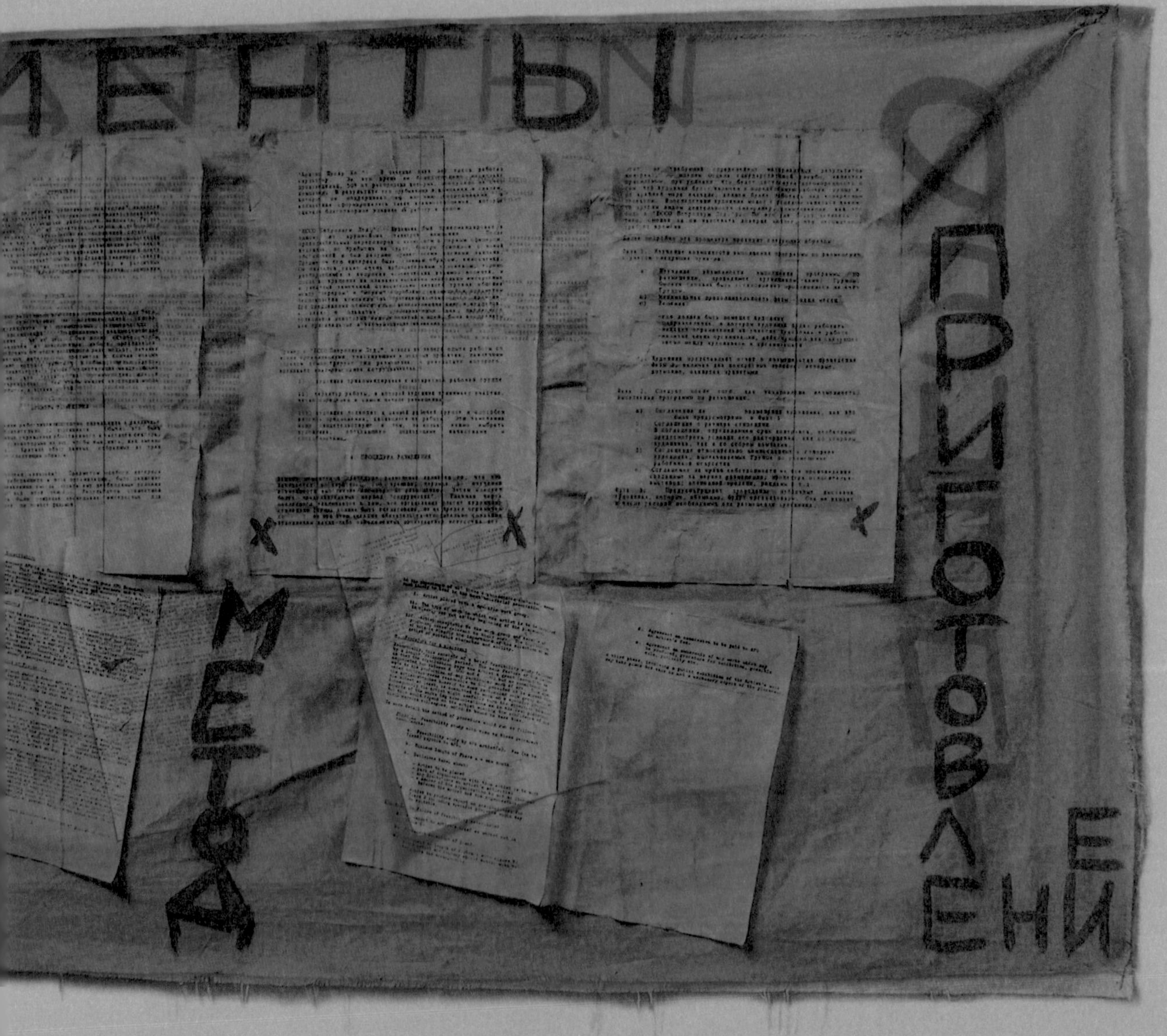

banner BANNER made for Borscht exhibition, St Petersburg (1993). Containing pages of APG's Civil Service Memorandum (1973) with Russian translations.

vision BANNER sent to Antagonismes exhibition at MACBA, Barcelona (2001) as a rolled up piece of un-stretched canvas.

product BANNER returned in a bespoke wooden shipping crate.

Repositioning Art in the Decision-Making Process of Society

Réseau pour la Remise en Place de l'Art dans le Processus de Prise de Décision par la Société

The overall objective of the network is to realign the artist's contribution in society to non-art contexts of government, commerce and other disciplines, in recognition that the future must involve a more integrated and comprehensive approach to political and social organisations, in which the insight of artists has a significant role to play.

Co-ordinator
Barbara Steveni

- To promote and protect creative quality and initiatives from possible erosion and misrepresentation through bureaucratic processes within art institutions, art education and non-art organisations,

Redacted page from 'Arts Networking in Europe', 1997

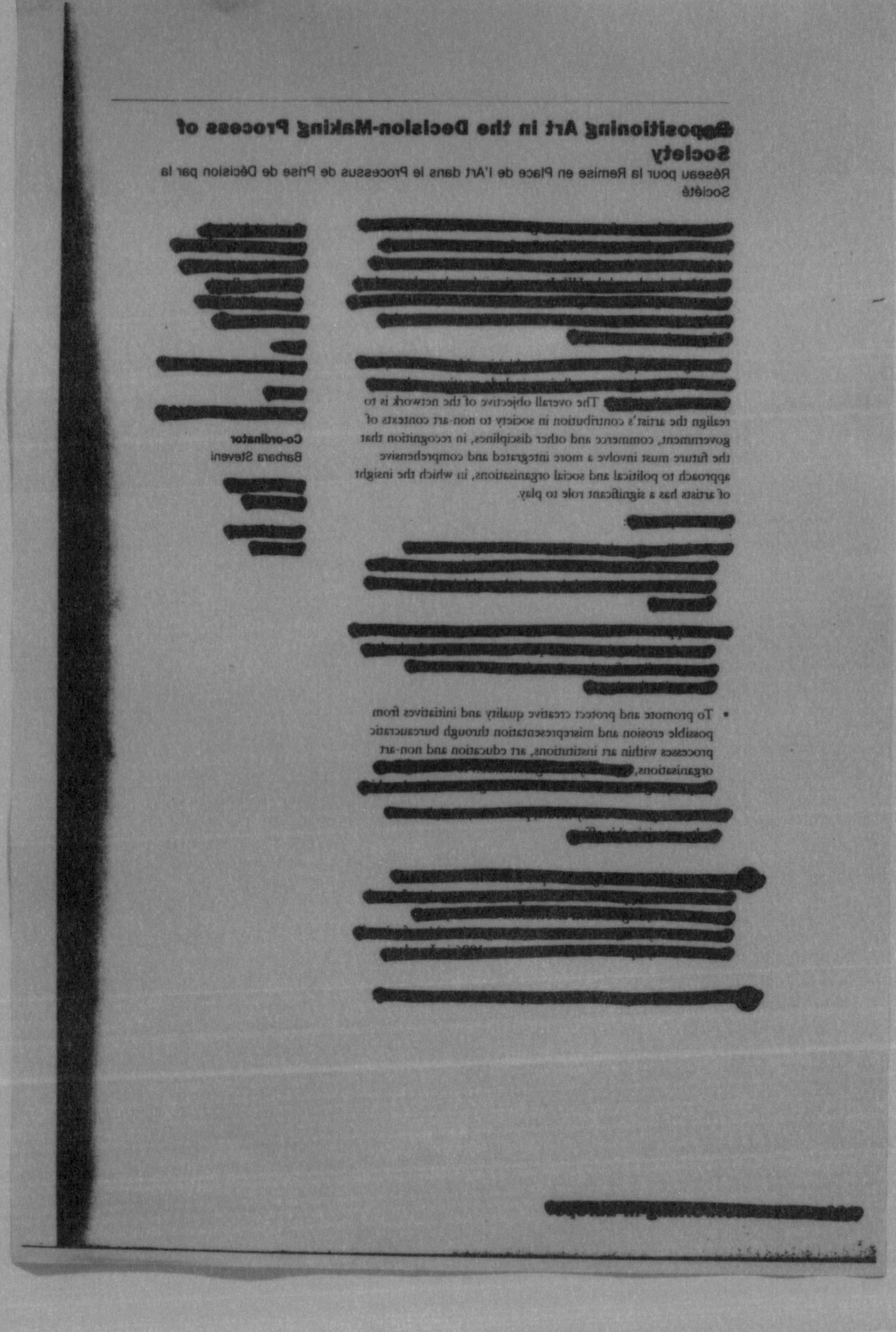

Repositioning Art in the Decision-Making Process of Society

Réseau pour la Remise en Place de l'Art dans le Processus de Décision par la Société

The overall objective of the network is to realign the artist's contribution in society to non-art contexts of government, commerce and other disciplines, in recognition that the future must involve a more integrated and comprehensive approach to political and social organisations, in which the insight of artists has a significant role to play.

- To promote and protect creative quality and initiatives from possible erosion and misrepresentation through bureaucratic processes within art institutions, art education and non-art organisations.

Co-ordinator
Barbara Steveni

In the 60's I made a painting on the back of a discarded John Latham canvas, which he had liked very much. I asked myself recently where value lay: in my painting as John had bestowed, in our now double-sided canvas, or the Latham reject?

In the 60's I made a painting on the back of a discarded John Latham canvas, which he had liked very much. I asked myself recently where value lay: in my painting as John had bestowed, in our now double-sided canvas, or the Latham reject?

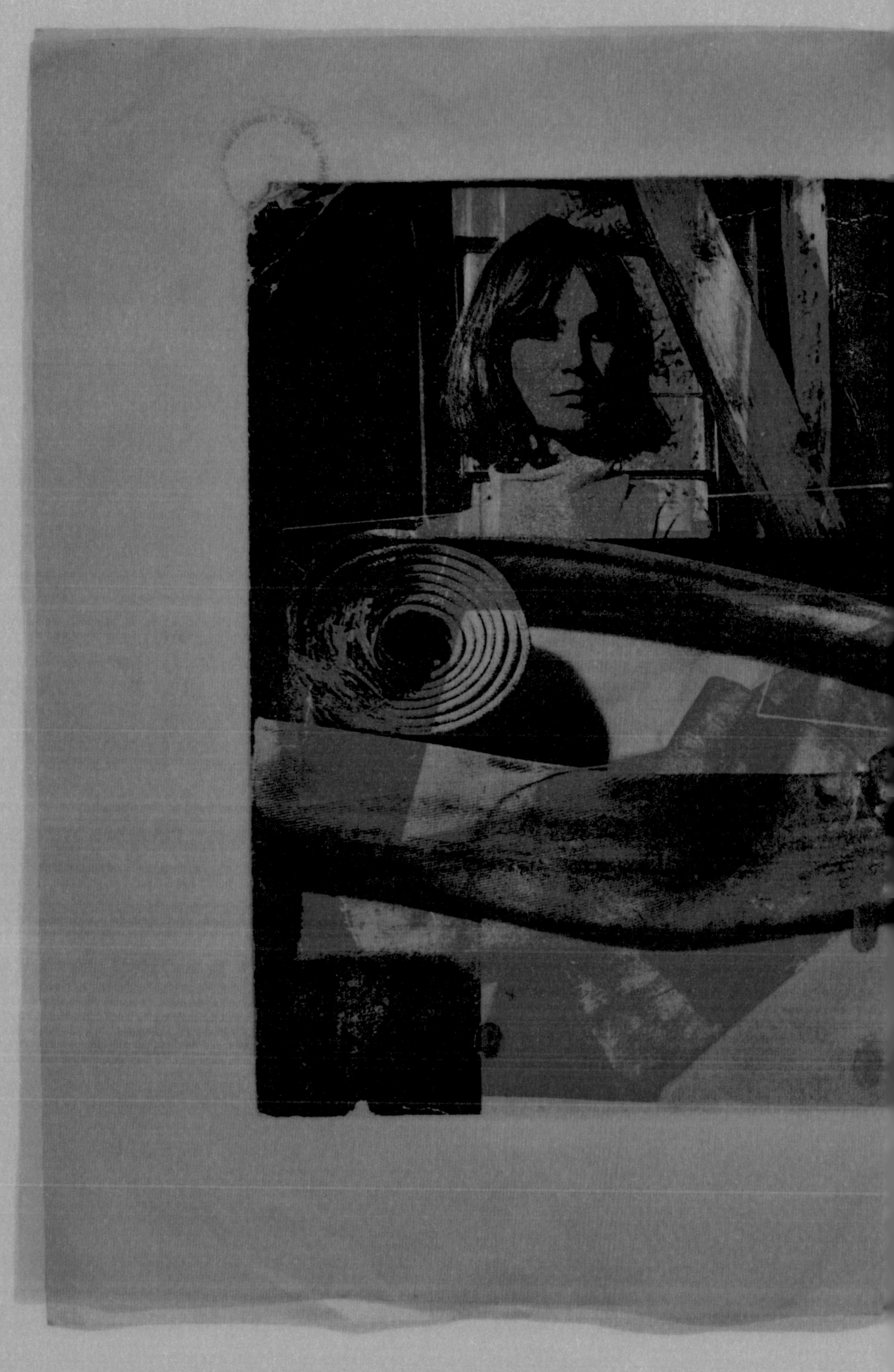

A 1964 portrait of Barbara Steveni with assemblage, photographed by Jorge Lewinski. The original print is held in the APG collection at Tate Archive. Portrait © The Lewinski Archive at Chatsworth / Bridgeman Images

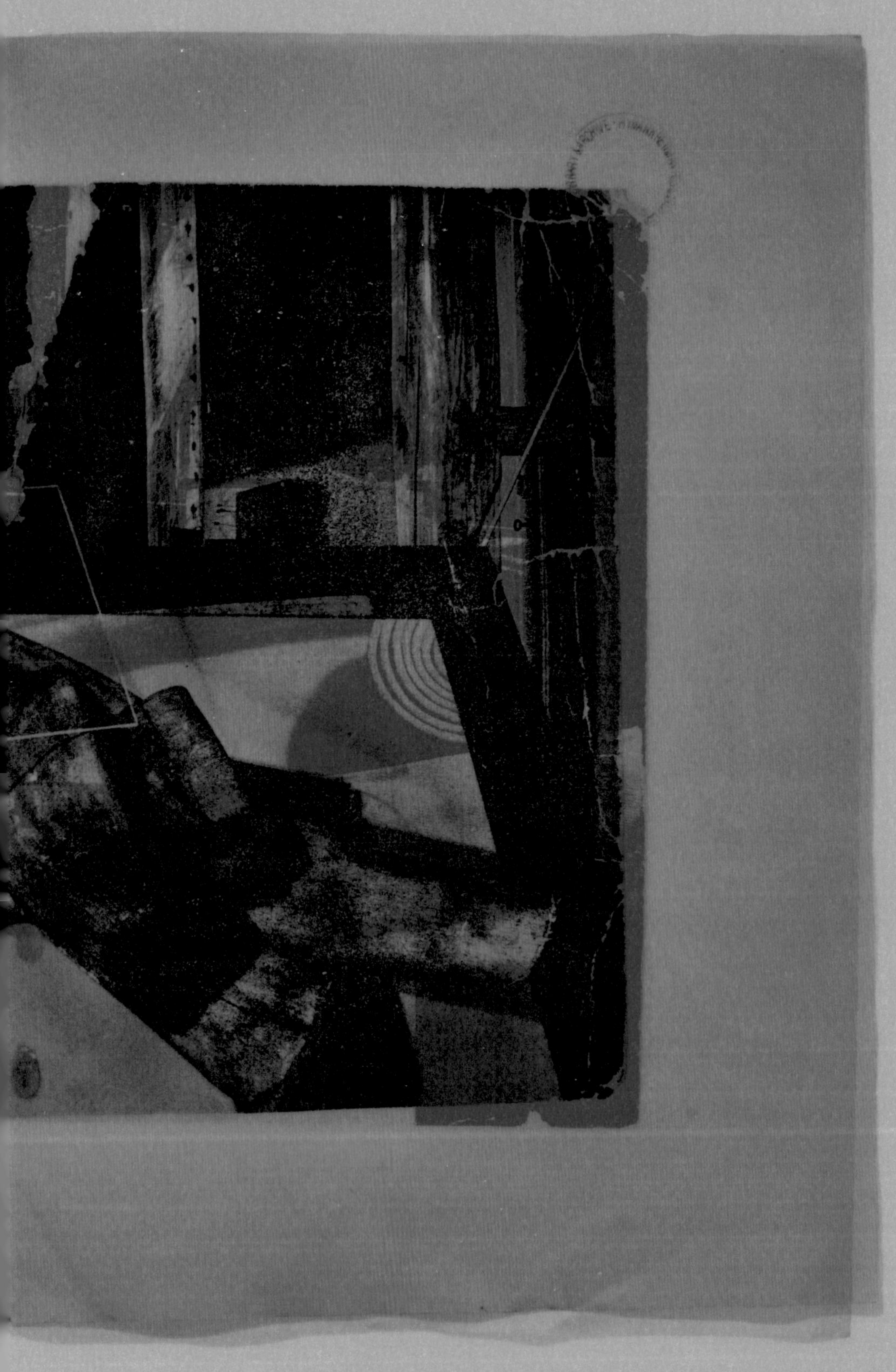

A 1964 portrait of Barbara Steveni with assemblage, photographed by Jorge Lewinski. The original print is held in the APG collection at Tate Archive. Portrait © The Lewinski Archive at Chatsworth / Bridgeman Images

By 'instituting' yourself, you
have a level of equivalence
with the organisations you're
working with, that perhaps as
an individual artist you don't
have. By coming together under
a name, you have a better basis
on which to negotiate with large
institutions.

John Hill, Instituted by Artists, June 2012

The government says to us
that philanthropy is a good
thing ... but the problem is that
it transfers power away from
public institutions, distorts
their mission and persuades
them to behave like private
institutions.

Bob and Roberta Smith, What are we worth?
Artists and the Economic Crisis, October 2011

Courtney J. Martin in conversation
with Gilane Tawadros

Making it in the USA: a conversation on art and culture

Gilane Tawadros The US model of arts funding is one that is being used by the current government as the ideal model for philanthropy for the arts. Thinking specifically about the US context, how would you say artists are valued? How does the public in the USA perceive artists?

Courtney J. Martin From the US context, is there a national conversation about art and artists? I think that there is a cultural sector (public and non-profit arts institutions, art schools or government-funded arts programmes, for example) and that there is a popular understanding of what art might be in the USA. These are two very different things.

From a US perspective, I would say that artists, as individuals, do not actually count in how the public perceives of the States. Art is not a constituent part of any kind of economic market that we have in play. I do not think people in the USA have come to a national consensus about artists as professional entities or about art as a result of a professional interaction. When the knowledge of the art market, or what some might call the 'art world', intersects with public discourse, it is completely illuminating for both sides, such as the infamous theft of Old Master and Impressionist works from the Isabella Stewart Gardner Museum on 19 March 1990. That case radiated out of both the local environment of Boston and cohorts of arts professionals to gain national attention in the press, in numerous narrativised prime-time television accounts and in a *New York Times* best-selling book.[1] And, yet, it is the inflammatory, spectacle quality of this event that is pursued in the public, not one of art and its value to the institution (the Gardner) or the city (Boston) and certainly not the larger industry of which it is a part.

GT How does art enter public discourse on an everyday basis?

CJM There are very few media outlets in which art can be brought to the mainstream on a regular, non-exceptional, basis. The *New York Times*, of course, has a regular section on art and artists that reviews contemporary and historical exhibitions and highlights current trends, as well as profiling contemporary artists. By the same token, the *Los Angeles Times* made redundant their art reporter in a sweep of staff reductions in 2013. Neither publication stages art in terms of a market analysis, in the manner accorded to other commodities. If the *Times* on both coasts are seen as a barometer of a general interest in art, then we are lopsided. If you wanted to know more about art and artists, you would have to go to a specialist publication, but how would you know about that specialist publication without wider circulation? So, in the bigger picture, there is no national value attached to the economy of art or artists.

GT Was there a public response to the extinguishing of art reporting in the *Los Angeles Times*?

CJM The response was a letter to the editor signed by several museum directors from southern California. Their chief response was that art drove the economy in the region. This is certainly true in specific cities across the country that serve as 'micro sites' or 'small cases' of creative economies.

GT Cities, for example, like Miami?

CJM Miami, absolutely Miami. So, Miami gets to benefit from the biggest slice of the art market pie that is visible both to the art world and to the population of the city. Its success is an anomaly, but there are art fairs throughout the country that function as regional arms of the larger art market. Chicago has had an art fair since 1980, which declined, became defunct for a few years and re-emerged in 2013 under new direction as *Expo Chicago*. Similarly, Los Angeles has an emergent art fair – *Art Los Angeles Contemporary* – and a well-established photography fair, the *Annual International Los Angeles Photographic Art Exposition*, aka *Photo LA*.

GT What I think you're saying is that there is a disconnect between the public valuation of art and artists on a national level and then specific geographies and economies where actual art and artists play a very significant part ...

CJM Absolutely. I think there is a sense that art and artists have value but I do not think that cities or states have figured out how to harness that value in any comprehensive way. And since these events, like fairs, happen at a 'local' level of city or region, there is not a national conversation about the market of art comparable to those around financial or real estate markets. These markets receive and generate a great deal of attention and speculation. If that lens were turned onto art as a productive sector, perhaps it would change public discourse about art and artists.

GT So, thinking about this in a more historical context, recent history that is, what have been the significant changes do you think in the way that artists are valued and validated now compared with how they have been valued and validated over the past decade? Do you perceive any milestones or any significant shifts?

CJM Well, let me go back to an understanding of what happened after the Second World War. If, as Serge Guilbaut proposed, Paris was the epicentre of an artistic and cultural life that sustained the world before the war,[2] amid the upheaval in Europe, the war destroyed Paris's hold on culture and, ultimately, precipitated the relocation of art (as one cultural form) to New York. The USA, by way of New York, received important immigrant artists, critics, art historians, dealers and patrons. From that point on, New York was recognised as the new place to make, show and sell art.

What Guilbaut does not say, however, is that for all of the art world that decamped from Paris to New York, the one thing that did not go was the knowledge of how to support art and artists nationally. So, while we were perfectly happy to become a centre of culture, the USA did not inherit a framework for how to support the individual entities (artists, art schools, institutions, etc.) that make a culture. For example, people in the USA learn quickly to collect, but only sporadically is patronage passed on – and collecting and patronage are very different things. Similarly, the government does not take on artists' subsidies, housing or studios as a function of the state, although many cities have benefited from groupings of the creative class.

The USA never learned these lessons. If you then move forward by 50 to 60 years, art and the nation are in exactly the same places as they were after the war. In that time, the art market has shifted to other places. From 1988, or so, London reasserted itself as an international contemporary art market, full of both producers (artists) and consumers (museum goers, collectors, etc.). In the decade that followed, other cities, such as Hong Kong, Dubai and Delhi, entered the market. One might look at all of these markets as part of a shift necessitated by the USA not having made the proper investment in culture in the previous 50 years.

GT I'm interested in this idea of a national narrative about the value of art. Taking your starting point in the post-war era, I am thinking about how Abstract Expressionist painters were folded into a narrative of US political freedom and a narrative of the USA as a world leader in terms of its political system and by extension its economic system. And yet the trajectory of an increasingly global art world has actually resulted in people collecting and investing their money in artworks that follow specific identities and cultural affiliations. So, for example, one of the big drivers for the Indian art market in its fledgling state, two decades ago, was the investment by Indian/US collectors who were buying works in Delhi by some of the great modernist Indian painters.

CJM Exactly.

GT In some ways, it's easier to see the value that the market confers on the work of an artist, which then translates into commercial value and is reflected in the increased prices that an artist can command in the market. I think what's less obvious, perhaps, is the value that curatorial practice and art historical research and writing bring through validation. Can you say something about your experience of this?

CJM Let me add one more thing in there. I think that critical practices should be brought in as well, so the writing of art criticism should be something that is on a par with the way that one looks at what affects the perception of artists. Unfortunately, criticism does not exist as a function of the market.

Again, if we go back to the post-Second World War period, criticism was the thing that sat between the artist and her/his market value. One needed critics to discuss art; even if they hated it, it was still promotion. Now there is no real criticism.

GT So, if critique and validation no longer come via art criticism because that no longer exists, do they come through scholarship and curation in public institutions, let's say?

CJM The rising mis-use of the term 'curator' is directly related to the demise of criticism. Twenty years ago, many people who call themselves curators now might have defined themselves as critics or as art writers, had the tenets around these terms remained critically rigorous.

As an art historian who has worked as a curator and as a critic, I think that the rise of 'curator' as a title is tied to what the market 'sees'. Does our history have anything to do with this? In terms of actual market value, curatorial practice has more of a public face as a disseminator of art history. Perhaps this is why many art historians who once assumed that curatorial work was a lesser practice, and a less prestigious field, have now taken on curatorial practice. I am glad that the hierarchy between the academy and the museum is deteriorating. The museum is where art history is applied for the general public and one of the places people are shaped as cultural beings. Simultaneously, museum education has been one of the chief areas of expansive thinking in the last 30 years. Education programmes within museums often push their institutions to take on serious questions and truly develop audiences. Some of the most avant-garde practices in museology happen in education departments, or as an outgrowth of museum pedagogy. It is the education department that interacts with all sectors of the public: from school children to retirees. It is not by accident that education departments employ working artists and have economically and racially diverse staff, when compared to the corpus of the museum.

GT Has the money flowed out of the academy and into the museum? Has the balance of economic power between those two spaces shifted so that the money now resides and opportunity resides within the museum rather than the academy in the USA?

CJM For those of us who study art history and pursue the field professionally, the range of information that we have is vast. We are rigorous readers and writers, sleuths set onto objects in search of minute detail. We are responsible for multiple languages, political, social and cultural histories, alongside deep economic analytical tools, not to mention some aspects of science relative to material considerations. To know art history is to move between the micro and macro of an object and its origins in all possible manners.

The perception of the field is, of course, flat. It is either invisible or a kind of foil for the class, race and gender assumptions that, sadly, still pervade the field. Since 2008, and the ensuing economic crises, the problem of art history has been part and parcel of a general dismissal of the humanities that echoes through the academy. I do not think, however, that the funding of secondary education and the funding for museums is interrelated now or ever; rarely do the two meet, despite the philanthropic connections that are common to many areas of American life. Historically, universities and museums have benefited from similar donor bases, but so have hospitals, libraries and public parks.

GT And have you seen any shifts in the patterns of philanthropic patronage in the USA over the past decade?

CJM Yes, many of the major philanthropies that funded art began to weaken after 2000. In their wake, the new foundations, such as the Bill and Melinda Gates Foundation started in 1997, have tended to fund other sectors: health, education, financial reform, for example. There does seem to be a palpable split between old and new, wherein art, primarily its institutions, is receiving far fewer resources and far less money.

GT So has that created a gap and a vacuum in terms of private patronage and direct support for artists?

CJM No, because there was never the expectation in the USA that artists were going to receive individual funding from foundations. The gap is actually with institutions, so art museums receive far less money than they previously did. Very little of that money passed down to individual artists anyway; most of it

went to exhibitions and general operations, which is why museums suffer
so much because no-one wants to contribute to general operating funds.

GT And what has been the impact of the cuts to the National Endowment
for the Arts (NEA)?

CJM From the 1990s, public funding for the arts became a highly scrutinised,
political issue, one that seemed to target artists and institutions disproportionately
at the margins of art's financial largess. In 1998, Senator Jesse Helms condemned
the use of public funds for art after viewing Andres Serrano's photograph, *Piss
Christ* (1987), in an exhibition at the Southeastern Center for Contemporary Art
in Winston-Salem, North Carolina. North Carolina was Helms's home state and
the exhibition at the Center was funded by the NEA, thus Helms had both a local
(his constituency) and a federal (as a member of the Senate) stake in denouncing
Serrano, the show and its funding. Rightly or wrongly, this moment added to a
national conversation about public support of arts funding that would, ultimately,
also include the National Endowment for the Humanities (NEH). This battle in
the so-called 'culture wars' was in many ways just a partisan conflict between the
warring two-party political system, not unlike the recent feuding over healthcare
reform or school nutrition. The real impact of this now 20-year-old saga has been
to, effectively, sideline a national arts agenda. The NEA is still involved in arts
funding, nationally and internationally, but the perception of its import is
diminished, although, in fact, it was never a significant source of national funding.
    Seen from another vantage, Helms's, and others', citation for indecency against
Serrano is part of a larger, public conversation about gender and sexuality. In
that way, it proves, yet again, that art is often the catalyst for real engagement
with important issues.

GT I'm going to start winding up our conversation, Courtney, but I want to give
you the opportunity either to crystal ball gaze or to comment on anything that
I haven't directly invited you to comment on that you want to say in relation
to these questions around the economy of art and patronage in the US context ...

CJM Earlier you asked for examples of artists that have achieved significant
critical acclaim but have failed to achieve financial success. Sure, this happens
a lot. The mythology of the poor artist resounds throughout contemporary art
discourse. I think that the more pressing concern for making art in the USA
is the uneven healthcare system. Anecdotally, I know lots of artists that are able
to support themselves and grow their practices from the sales of their work, but

they either spend a disproportionate amount of their total income on private health insurance or they rely on a secondary job (or the job of a spouse) solely for the insurance benefit. It seems almost trite to raise this issue, but the thing that separates the USA from its European counterparts is universal access to medical care.

So, the job itself funds the health insurance but just that time spent doing something else puts a kind of crippling effect onto the crafters or they are spending an inordinate amount of money paying out of pocket for health insurance, which still does not guarantee full coverage. It is a very precarious situation to find yourself in if you have children or dependants or if you make work that requires physicality, like performance. To return to the idea of the market, a single artist is a kind of small business that can support a whole ecosystem (their families, their neighbours, any number of workers and other craft makers and technicians, etc.). To stymie that possibility is to inhibit entrepreneurship on multiple levels. There is a common concern that people in the USA no longer 'make' anything, since so much factory production has been outsourced internationally and agriculture is not encouraged. Yet, we have only recently, by way of the tech industries, begun a conversation about what this kind of change would require. Access to affordable healthcare is a significant constituent in this issue. It is a particularly US problem to be financially viable but utterly unable to take care of yourself in terms of health, but it is one that US artists (and any artist that desires to work in the USA) face daily. When Berlin began to attract more young artists in the late 1990s, one of the primary features that defined this trend was access to affordable healthcare. Another reason was state-supported, or subsidised, studio space.

GT I'm so glad that you raised this issue because I think that a lot of people here, particularly politicians, look over the pond and see the USA as an ideal context for artists and art, and issues like access to healthcare and studio space are ones that we don't often consider.

1   See Ulrich Boser, *The Gardner Heist: The True Story of the World's Largest Unsolved Art Theft* (New York: HarperCollins, 2009)
2   Serge Guilbaut and Arthur Goldhammer (trans.), *How New York Stole the Idea of Modern Art: Abstract Expressionism, Freedom and the Cold War* (Chicago: University of Chicago, 1983)

In terms of public funding, there's more money for the arts in the UK than there ever has been before … . We're used to talking about how we don't spend enough money on the arts in the UK, but in fact we're actually spending a hell of a lot. However bad it gets, and however much that is reduced, it's being reduced from a much higher level than we might have been at 20 years ago.

John Kieffer, What are we worth? Artists and the Economic Crisis, October 2011

Two or three years ago, when the recession first started to really take hold, I was worried by the amount of commercially represented artists and commercial gallery logos that were appearing on touring or major institutional shows. Now, I am slightly more at home with it, because this is the way that many international institutions have worked for a long time. They don't have the level of public subsidy we do [in the UK], so they have relied on patrons, collectors or commercial galleries to effectively support the major shows. It's not a problem as long as there are emerging curators, facilitators, organisations that support unrepresented artists, or at least advise them. If institutions that are benefiting from the corporate and commercial sectors are also investing time and energy in supporting unrepresented artists, then it's not as big a problem as it could be.

Matt Roberts, Market Matters, March 2012

The audience for the big public institutions in this country is growing. That's about the public realm, and is a very important thing for artists to realise. Their authority, the authority of art, exists through this conversation that we can all have, not the conversation that the elite can have [which is] meaningless. The conversation that we all have within the public realm is something to celebrate and that's one of the things that we ought to be fighting for.

Bob and Roberta Smith, What are we worth?
Artists and the Economic Crisis, October 2011

Works can sell for a huge amount of money, and are prestige symbols, just as when an Ashanti chief commissioned a mask for a dance; it's always a status thing to have whatever your society calls the best art. That seems to be universal; that's not the problem. The problem is that there is an absolute conflation of economic and intrinsic value in art. When people started saying to me about ten to twelve years ago, 'Oh, I'm so excited about art!' I said: 'No you're not. You're excited about money.' So art becomes just a token of the money, and that is harsh for artists.

Susan Hiller, The Economy of Art, November 2009

John Kieffer

Funny business

In 1989 I arrived for my first day at work as Arts Development Manager for the
London Docklands Development Corporation (LDDC). I was almost literally
clueless as to what to do. The LDDC was a free enterprise zone created by Margaret
Thatcher's government in 1981 to 'regenerate' the Docklands area of East and
South-East London. Eight years into the life of the LDDC, and only five years
away from when the process of withdrawal was due to start, the combined
forces of an enabling government and the market had delivered a great deal
of infrastructure and plenty of steel + glass + atrium office buildings but had
failed to 'deliver arts and culture' to either the newly relocated Yuppies and
Sloane Rangers or the dislocated working-class communities of London's old
East End. Indeed much of what constituted vernacular or contemporary culture
in that part of London was flattened (temporarily at least) by the monetarist
steamroller. Olympia & York, the original commercial developer of Canary
Wharf on the Isle of Dogs, had come to a similar view as the LDDC and had
instigated its own arts events and commissioning programme.

Day one and I already had a meeting in the diary with two artists called
Damien Hirst and Billee Sellman. My assistant warned me that 'they're very nice
but they're quite pushy!' They were indeed both of those things. The meeting took
place and a smallish grant was arranged towards what would become the 1990
exhibition *Modern Medicine* at Building One, Bermondsey. Suddenly I was no
longer clueless as to what a large part of my work over the next two years would
entail. I would fairly shamelessly base much of the LDDC's arts programme on
what we now see as the beginning of the young British artists (yBa) movement.[1]

As a temporary exile from the (relatively) straightforward world of music, and
at the time a newcomer to the world of the visual arts, I remember looking around
the attendees at the dinner following the *Modern Medicine* exhibition and, having
spotted only a few familiar faces, I asked an artist friend who everyone else was:
'They're mostly dealers. They basically own everyone here or will do by the end
of the evening.'

This essay is a personal view of the last 25 years of public funding for the
contemporary visual arts, the relationship between artists, public funding and
the art market, and some thoughts about how things could be different. I have
chosen this time span largely because I have been there or thereabouts as an
interested outsider for most of this period. I have not attempted to map out the
crucial artist-dealer-collector relationship that has been covered extensively
elsewhere,[2] and similarly I mostly avoid looking at the role of intermediaries
such as critics and curators.

The picture in the late 1980s to the early 1990s (by which time I had moved
to the then new London Arts Board[3]) was one of the larger publicly-funded

galleries already committed to showing the contemporary visual arts,[4] along with a growing number of new smaller-scale funded spaces,[5] and a then burgeoning group of unruly and much-missed artist-run spaces.[6] This period also saw artists having the opportunity to increasingly work outside the gallery environment in public and found spaces through new commissioning organisations[7] and the more formal 'public art' sector, which had moved into overdrive due, in part, to the 1980s property development boom.[8] The first wave of community arts organisations formed in the 1960s and 1970s, whose practice was based in the visual arts, were in a state of flux prompted to some extent by funding cuts (many of which were implemented while I was at the London Arts Board). Perhaps the most significant change in the funding landscape during this period was the range of culturally diverse practice that followed the Black Arts Movement of the 1980s, which began to gain a foothold on the funding ladder.[9] Support for individual artists was hard to find with the odd funding scheme administered by the public funding bodies and a handful of trusts and foundations. In London at least, the studio organisations Acme and Space skilfully worked with and against the grain of the development game to create new accommodation for artists, in the former case incorporating living space.

Last, but certainly not least, the Tate in particular carefully tracked all of the various themes and tendencies in the contemporary visual arts and, as if paving the way for the arrival of its big sister, Tate Modern, increasingly reflected within its walls what was happening outside of them.

Elsewhere the 'floating crap game'[10] that constitutes the art market had gone through its own period of boom and (relative) bust and was keenly eyeing up the contemporary visual arts for its next phase of growth. The action was also starting to move away from Cork Street and its environs with independent artists, dealers and collectors opening highly significant contemporary art spaces in the early 1990s.[11]

As a funder during this period, the London Arts Board was very much concerned with helping create something akin to an ecosystem for the visual arts: something that would expand opportunities for artists to make high-quality work and for the public to experience the work in a wide range of settings; something that was responsive to new practice rather than buoyed along by inertia; and something that fitted together and made a certain kind of sense. We were, of course, aware of curators, but the phenomenon of curator-as-superstar was still a few years ahead, and did not particularly shift our focus away from artists and buildings.

It is almost impossible to imagine funders behaving in this way today, but we were undoubtedly change junkies, deeply suspicious of anything that looked

like the status quo and determined to fix it. If anything we were guilty of trying
to alter too much too fast, and the shifts in spending in all of the art forms, not
least the visual arts, although small compared with today were very significant
at the time. While most of the changes held, the organisation itself buckled
under external pressure and was eventually merged (back) into the Arts Council.

I was very aware of the role of the commercial music industry, West End theatre
and the publishing industry, but I was hopelessly naïve at the time about the role
of the art market in relation to the visual arts. Despite what should have been
a wake-up call at *Modern Medicine* a few years before, it was still 'over there
somewhere' and had little to do with how we allocated public money.

So what has changed over the last 25 years?
To a great extent the template for funding the contemporary visual arts was cut
in the late 1980s and it seems that we are living with the model. In one sense
almost everything has got much bigger – buildings, audiences, media coverage
and the reputations of many artists. And yes, there has been some reshuffling
of personnel, a few institutional and individual arrivals and departures, but it
all feels very familiar.

Most areas of the arts coexist with the commercial sector as part of everyday
reality, and commercial realities are faced by everyone from individual artists
to major cultural institutions. But is there a relationship as shrouded in mystery
as the one between the publicly-funded visual arts and the art market?

I should be clear about what I mean by the art market. It is an international
industry with a turnover of just under £40 billion with a growth rate running
at 8%. According to the International Monetary Fund that is roughly the
equivalent of the Gross Domestic Product of Sri Lanka. The UK has a 20%
market share – £8 billion – and that is over three times the combined budgets
of the English, Welsh, Scottish and Northern Irish culture departments.

What does this proximity mean?
The traditional stance of the funding agencies has been to celebrate the
success of the UK contemporary art market as a positive outcome of public
funding and to welcome its 'unprecedented support for UK visual artists to
develop international careers.'[12] It would be churlish to deny the tax revenues,
jobs, tourists and hotel beds that flow from such a financial powerhouse, but
has this relationship done anything to improve the structural problems within
the visual arts in the UK, or when a beast is this big, even something more?
What is in it for artists and for the public?

Artists, of course, are not made. They make themselves. But along the way
they benefit from the different phases of education, and if they are lucky and
very good they also benefit from support from publicly-funded galleries and

other institutions. Then, if they are very lucky indeed, they can make a lot of money for themselves, dealers and collectors. The fact that the vast majority of artists do not make the transition to mega-riches is not the point here. It is more fundamental than that. The contemporary visual arts have ended up trapped in a system where success is partly defined through the conversion of unquantifiable creative work not just into products but also into tradable assets. There is nothing new here of course. It is capitalism, stupid! But it is a particularly brutish version of capitalism that brings little or no benefit to the vast majority of its workforce. At a time when public arts funding increasingly describes itself as 'investment', is it not time to 'follow the money trail'?

It would not be unreasonable to expect that artists themselves are benefiting from both feeding a multi-billion pound industry and from what has until recently been an exponential rise in public funding. Not a chance. As we know from the recent *Paying Artists* report and associated campaign, 71% of artists receive no fee for publicly-funded exhibitions and nearly 60% do not even have their expenses covered.[13]

And then there is the public to consider. With national lottery funds increasingly being used to replace government funding, how long is it before someone asks whether it is right for the poorest people in the country to subsidise a system where the artists who make the stuff are often not paid, and that feeds a market populated almost entirely by the super-rich?

It would be wrong, however, to blame the market for this strange state of affairs. There is a value system at work in the arts that has coalesced almost by stealth over the last 30 years. Very few people, if any, who work in the sector would agree with it – but almost all of us collude with it.

The value system is a contradictory mush of managerialism, boosterism, paternalism and neoliberalism. That is a lot of -isms, but what does it look and feel like? Maybe something like this:

- An outdated top-down funding system based on competition between artists and organisations rather than collaboration and cooperation.

- Organisations with a governance structure more suited to the nineteenth century than the twenty-first.

- With artists increasingly required to subsidise both themselves and the venues that show their work, all aspects of the visual arts profession will continue to be the preserve of the middle-class metropolitan elite.

- A profession that has become too professional, and where everyone apart from the artists is thriving. First there were arts managers – now everyone is either a leader or a curator.

- A sector where public funding is in danger of becoming a proxy for public engagement, audiences replace people and tickets replace relationships. We are all marketeers now.

- A defensive public discourse dominated by advocacy-speak. Are we really that good all the time?

- A spectacularly wonky economic model where public investment benefits a handful of artists and a lot of hedge-fund managers.[14]

So what can be done? Imagining an alternative to how things are has become almost impossible. Where is the incentive for change? Over the years, funding cuts have largely been met by funding bodies tinkering with the 'portfolio' rather than a wholesale rethink, and the pressure to keep things as close to the status quo as possible is enormous. I know, I've been there.

The art market is beyond our reach, at least for the moment, but I believe that we can and should start to re-imagine how public funding for the visual arts could be better. Given the gravitational pull of business-as-usual for most institutions and funders, the impetus for change is more likely to come from artists themselves looking outside of the funding system for new models and thinking that challenge both the logic of the market and the logjam of public subsidy.

We could start by asking ourselves some questions:

- What would a visual arts economy that primarily brought benefits to artists and the public look like?

- Many artists operate within barter, timebanking and other informal exchange and support networks. Could these networks become a bottom-up system for the distribution of public funding for artists?

- What can we learn from initiatives such as crowdfunding? Could this be a basis for different kinds of relationships with audiences and the public?

- What can we learn from new models of social enterprise, local currencies, community economies etc. that exist outside of the arts?

- Do those with power in the visual arts spend too much time trying to influence politicians and not enough time talking to the public?

- Do artists in receipt of public funding have the right not to care about the public?

- At a time when public space is increasingly privatised, galleries and visual arts spaces are a crucial part of a shrinking public realm. What more can we do to create relationships with the public apart from putting on shows?

- Artists are both the victims and unwilling agents of gentrification in our cities. What kind of external alliances can be made to build the arts into regeneration without the social cleansing that goes with it?

- We talk a lot about the economic impact of the arts but what more can we do to understand and communicate the social relations that allow artists to work and thrive and the benefits that they bring in return?[15]

- The public do not understand what we do and may not rush to our defence if the chips are down. Can we find new ways to tell the story about what artists do without getting our cues from academic language, Treasury handbooks, social work manuals or celebrity culture

- Many artists believe that what they do and how they work points towards a different way of living. Could we have more influence over the wider society and culture than we do at present?[16]

There are no simple answers to any of these questions, and the demands of day-to-day survival for organisations and artists will always trump time spent thinking about the big picture. If we do nothing, however, and the wider political context continues down its present track, I believe that the arts and artists will become increasingly marginalised and our world will start to look more and more like the luxury goods industry than something rooted in peoples' hearts and minds. Many years ago, at a meeting with the Arts Council, the writer and musician David Toop warned a group of his peers against becoming lost in a 'culture of enfeeblement'. At a time when arts funding is under attack, arts education is being decimated and we seem to have drifted from a market economy to a market society,[17] I believe that we should be brave and not feeble, and be more ambitious about the role of the visual arts and artists in society.

1   *Modern Medicine, Gambler*, Henry Bond
    and Sarah Lucas's *East Country Yard Show*,
    the Wise Taylor Partnership's *Next Phase*
    show and many others
2   Simon Knell (ed.), *Museums in the Material World*
    (Abingdon and New York: Routledge, 2007)
3   Alongside a remarkable range of colleagues
    – Stephen Beddoe, Sheena Etches, Amanda King,
    Mariam Sharp, and Holly Tebbutt, among others
4   Whitechapel, Arnolfini, Serpentine, Ikon, etc.
5   Matts, Showroom, Chisenhale, etc.
6   BANK, City Racing, Cubitt, etc.
7   Artangel and Locus+
8   Public Art Development Trust, Public
    Art Commissioning Agency, etc.
9   Iniva, Autograph ABP and others
10 William J. Baumol, 'Unnatural Value: Or
    Art Investment as Floating Crap Game',
    The American Economic Review, vol.76,
    issue 2, May 1986, pp.10–14
11 Saatchi, Interim Art, White Cube, etc.
12 *Turning Point: A Strategy for the Contemporary
    Visual Arts in England* (London: ACE, 2006)
13 www.payingartists.org.uk/wp-content/
    uploads/2014/05/Paying-Artists_Securing-
    a-future-for-visual-arts-in-the-UK_f.pdf
14 http://online.wsj.com/news/articles/SB1000142
    4052702303448204579337154245172202
15 Shelagh Wright et al., *The Art of Living
    Dangerously*, 2013, http://www.an.co.uk/
    publications/document/4313109
16 Charlie Tims and Shelagh Wright, *The Invisible
    Hand*, 2013, http://ietm.org/sites/default/files/
    invisible_hand.pdf
17 Michael Sandel, *What Money Can't Buy:
    The Moral Limits of Markets* (London: Allen
    Lane, 2012)

Acknowledgements
Thanks to Henrietta Norton for her thoughts
on crowdfunding and audiences, and to Peter
Jenkinson, Charlie Tims, Shelagh Wright and
the Johns Holden and Newbigin for their daily
shots of wisdom.

A market is a market, isn't it?
I remember the first piece of
work I sold. I remember the first
time someone put something
into auction; you felt that there
was some kind of betrayal. This
exchange went on where they
said they would look after it for
the rest of their lives; then of
course, two or three years later,
it goes to auction, and you take
it personally. Then the market
decides how much you're worth,
the value of your art at that
particular point in time.

Michael Landy, The Economy of Art, November 2009

You can't ignore the threats to teaching and to funding. Over the last ten years my income has come from a number of things: teaching, commissions, sales to institutions or private individuals; it's been a real rag bag. I should be very miserable about it all, but actually I think it's an interesting time: everything is in flux and there are going to be new opportunities which come out of that.

Simon Faithfull, Artists' Futures, February 2011

Sonia Boyce
Louisa Buck
Jeremy Deller
Alan Freeman
John Kieffer
Courtney J. Martin
Russell Martin
Keir McGuinness
Lynda Morris
Andrea Phillips
Barbara Steveni
Gilane Tawadros
Andrew Wheatley

Sonia Boyce

Sonia Boyce is a multimedia artist. After graduating from Stourbridge College of Art in 1983, she became a key figure in the British Black Arts Movement of the 1980s.

Through drawing, photography and collage, Boyce's early works tackled issues of race, gender and contemporary urban experience that question racial stereotypes in the media and everyday life in Britain. These pieces were often large, vibrant, chalk pastel drawings.

Since the 1990s, her practice has taken on a collaborative and participatory approach. Where her earlier work explored individual experience, more recently it has shifted emphasis to a collective experience of contemporary culture that brings the audience into sharper focus. She works with artists, vocalists and audiences to create improvised and spontaneous collaborations, sometimes through singing or spoken word, often using drawing, print, photography, video and sound to make the artwork.

Boyce is a Professor in Fine Art at Middlesex University and a Chair in Black Art & Design at the University of the Arts London. She has exhibited extensively in the UK and internationally, and her work is held in several public collections. In the 1980s she was one of the youngest artists of her generation to have her work purchased by the Tate and was awarded an MBE in 2007 for services to art.

Louisa Buck

Louisa Buck is a writer and broadcaster on contemporary art. She has been London Contemporary Art Columnist for *The Art Newspaper* since 1997 and is a regular reviewer on BBC radio and TV, including Front Row, Nightwaves and BBC World Service. She writes a weekly visual arts column for the *Telegraph Luxury*.

Among her other outlets are *Vogue*, *Art Quarterly*, *Sotheby's Magazine* and the *Guardian*, and she is the author of a number of catalogue essays for institutions including Tate, Whitechapel Gallery, ICA, London, and the Stedelijk Museum in Amsterdam.

Her books include *Relative Values or What's Art Worth?*, co-authored with Philip Dodd (BBC Books, 1991); *Moving Targets 2: A User's Guide to British Art Now* (Tate, 2000); *Market Matters: The Dynamics of the Contemporary Art Market* (Arts Council England, 2004) and *Owning Art: The Contemporary Art Collector's Handbook*, co-authored with Judith Greer (Cultureshock Media, 2006). Her latest book, *Commissioning Contemporary Art: A Handbook for Curators, Collectors and Artists*, was published by Thames & Hudson in October 2012.

Buck was a judge for the 2005 Turner Prize.

Jeremy Deller

Jeremy Deller is an English conceptual artist. After studying Art History at the Courtauld Institute and at Sussex University he began making artworks in the early 1990s, often showing them outside of conventional galleries. His work – as an orchestrator, filmmaker, curator and cultural archivist – explores popular and traditional culture. He frequently collaborates with diverse groups, with people taking centre stage in the parades, processions, choreographed performances and documentaries that are a feature of his work.

He brings together the old and new: for the 1997 work *Acid Brass* he brought about an unexpected and unusual transcription of a number of acid house anthems for a traditional brass band, a juxtaposition that offered the possibility not just of a collision but of an interaction between the cultures represented by these distinctly different musical forms. Deller continued with this strategy of permissiveness in the *Folk Archive* project, begun in 1999 with Alan Kane. The artists described this work as a 'celebration of subjectivity', and underlined the authenticity of the archived objects and documents.

Deller has exhibited widely both in the UK and internationally and presented his *English Magic* exhibition in the British Pavilion at the Venice Biennale in 2013. In 2004 he won the Turner Prize for *Memory Bucket* (2003), a documentary about Texas.

Alan Freeman

Alan Freeman was an economist at the Greater London Authority between 2000 and 2011, where he wrote *Creativity: London's Core Business* and was lead author for *The Living Wage: towards a Fairer London* and *Measuring and Comparing World Cities*. He was seconded to the London Development Agency from 2008 to 2010, where he was lead author for *London: a Cultural Audit*, the predecessor of the *World Cities Cultural Report*.

During this time, he co-wrote a series of influential provocations on the economics of culture with Hasan Bakhshi, Radhika Desai, Graham Hitchen and Jason Potts, posted on the Mission Models Money website. He is a visiting Professor at London Metropolitan University and lives in Winnipeg, Canada.

With Radhika Desai, he co-edits the 'Future of World Capitalism' book series. With Hasan Bakhshi and Peter Higgs, he co-wrote NESTA's *Dynamic Mapping of the UK Creative Industries* (2013). With Andrew Kliman he co-founded the International Working Group on Value Theory and co-edits the new critical pluralist journal *Critique of Political Economy*. He is a special adviser to the World Cities Cultural Forum, and currently serves on the Board of the Winnipeg Symphony Orchestra, Manitobans for the Arts and the Winnipeg Video Pool. His public domain works are regularly posted on the Academia, Repec and Slideshare open access sites.

John Kieffer

John Kieffer is a writer, policy adviser, creative producer, lecturer, public speaker, mentor and consultant. He started out organising music and arts events in the basement of a bookshop in Brighton and now has over 30 years' experience in cultural policy, arts funding, programming, arts management, digital strategies, creative industries development and the music industry.

He is a co-director of John3Shelagh with Shelagh Wright, John Newbigin and John Holden, with whom he has edited *After The Crunch* (British Council and Creative & Cultural Skills, 2009) and *Creativity Money Love: Learning for the 21st Century* (Creative & Cultural Skills, 2011), and has made regular contributions to a-n The Artists Information Company and to Guardian Culture Professionals.

He has worked with and for everyone, from big ones like the British Council where he was Director Performing Arts and Head of Music, to little ones like the Arts Foundation where he was a Director. He was a trustee of Artsadmin, Artangel and the BBC Performing Arts Fund, and is currently chair of the Longplayer Trust and of creativity and learning organisation A New Direction. He is also an adviser to Transforming Tate Modern, Cafe Oto in Dalston, Artsadmin, London-based performance company Unfinished Business, audio-visual company Touch and many others.

Courtney J. Martin

Courtney J. Martin is an assistant professor in the History of Art and Architecture Department at Brown University, specialising in the modern and contemporary fields. She received a doctorate from Yale University in 2009 for her research on twentieth-century British art and architecture. She is the author of essays on the work of many contemporary artists, including Rasheed Araeen, Kader Attia, Rina Banerjee, Frank Bowling, Leslie Hewitt, Asger Jorn, Wangechi Mutu, Ed Ruscha and Yinka Shonibare.

Prior to Brown, she was an assistant professor in the History of Art Department at Vanderbilt University (2010–13); Chancellor's Postdoctoral Fellow in the History of Art at the University of California at Berkeley (2009–10); a fellow at the Getty Research Institute (2008–9); and a Henry Moore Institute Research Fellow (2007). She also worked in the media, arts and culture unit of the Ford Foundation in New York on an international arts portfolio. After leaving Ford, she served as a consultant for the Foundation's Gulf Coast Transformation Initiative and the Integrating the Arts and Education Initiative.

In 2012, she curated a Focus Display of Frank Bowling's paintings at Tate Britain: *Drop, Roll, Slide, Drip … Frank Bowling's Poured Paintings 1973–1978*. In 2014, she curated an exhibition, *Minimal Baroque: Post-Minimalism and Contemporary Art*, at Rønnebæksholm in Denmark. Currently, she is working on a manuscript about British art and politics after 1968 and co-editing a volume of essays on the Anglo-American art critic and curator Lawrence Alloway.

Russell Martin

Russell Martin is a graduate from The Glasgow
School of Art (1998) and Goldsmiths College (2008).
From initially working in gallery education, his
self-initiated projects include the peer mentoring
group Speakeasy (1999–2001), and the HÔTEL
BELLVILLE and Way East artists' project spaces
in Waterloo (2003–4) and Hackney Wick (2008).
He co-produced and presented *Show me the Monet*
and *For Love and Money*, two series for Resonance
104.4FM on artists, arts and the economy (2006).
He is a co-founder and one of the directors of
Rational Rec, the interdisciplinary social occasion
working nationally and internationally to commission
and present new works. As well as being part-time
programme manager of Artquest, he is currently chair
of the board at The Showroom and a member of the
board at artist-led gallery and studio organisation Block.

Keir McGuinness

Keir McGuinness is a management consultant who
for the past 14 years has specialised in working
with galleries, artists and creative businesses.

Formerly a company and commercial lawyer
with 25 years' experience of working with retail
clients, Keir is also, among other things, a former
trustee and chair of the trustees of the Whitechapel
Gallery, a former chair of the Patrons of New Art at
Tate Britain and a Turner Prize juror. He is currently
a trustee of the Chisenhale Gallery, of the Marie-
Louise von Motesiczky Charitable Trust and of the
Felix Trust. He is the chair of the Patrons of the Royal
Academy Schools, a patron of the British Museum
and vice-chair of the Public Monuments and
Sculpture Association.

Lynda Morris

Lynda Morris was born in Scotland in 1947 and has two children. She studied art in Canterbury and worked at the ICA, London, from 1969 to 1971. Her 1973 RCA thesis researched Art & Language, Joseph Beuys and The Projects Class. From 1971 to 1974 she worked for Nigel Greenwood and organised the *Book as Artwork 1960-72* exhibition with Germano Celant. She wrote for *Studio International*, *The Listener* and *Art Press*. She was Richard Hamilton's assistant for his 1973 Guggenheim exhibition.

As exhibition organiser at the Midland Group, Nottingham, 1976–79, she worked on *Towards Another Picture* with Andrew Brighton. For 19 years she organised *EAST International* in Norwich, with assistants including Tim Wilcox, Josephine Lanyon, Kirsty Ogg, Andy Hunt, Michelle Cotton and Kaavous Clayton. She organised *Picasso: Peace and Freedom* (Tate Liverpool, 2010), and is now working on Picasso and Africa after 1945. She curated *Vanley Burke: By the Rivers of Birminam* (mac birmingham, 2012), which travelled to Johannesburg in 2014.

She developed *Conception, the Conceptual Documents 1968-72* with Catherine Moseley (2000) and *Unconcealed: The International Network of Conceptual Artists 1967-1977* (Ridinghouse, 2009) from Sophie Richard's PhD. *Dear Lynda …*, commissioned by Matthew Higgs White Columns Gallery, New York, in 2012, travelled to Chelsea, Dundee, Norwich, Berlin and Birmingham. She has lectured at the Getty Museum (2009), LACMA (2012) and DIA Beacon (2014). She curated *Documenting Cadere 1972-78* (MOMA Oxford, 2012) and *Genuine Conceptualism* (Herbert Foundation, Ghent, 2014).

Andrea Phillips

Dr Andrea Phillips is professor of fine art and director of PhD programmes in the Art Department at Goldsmiths. She lectures and writes about the economic and social construction of publics within contemporary art.

Her current publications include *How To Work Together* (http://howtoworktogether.org/think-tank/andrea-phillips-how-to-work-together/, Chisenhale Gallery, The Showroom, Studio Voltaire, 2014), and contributions to the following publications: *Cluster: A Dialectionary* (Sternberg, 2014); *Economy: Art and the Subject after Postmodernism* (Liverpool University Press, 2014); *David Adjaye* (University of Chicago Press, 2014); *A Space Called Public* (Walter Koenig, 2013); *Architecture as Situation* (University of Edinburgh, 2013); and *Esther Shalev-Gerz: The Contemporary Art of Trusting Uncertainties and Unfolding Dialogues* (Art & Theory, 2013).

Recent and ongoing research projects include: *Curating Architecture*, a think-tank and exhibition examining the role of exhibitions in the making of architecture's social and political forms (Arts & Humanities Research Council (AHRC), 2007–9; *Actors, Agent and Attendants*, a research project and set of publications that address the role of artistic and curatorial production in contemporary political milieus (in collaboration with Stichting Kunst en Openbare Ruimte (SKOR), 2009–12; co-director with Suhail Malik, Andrew Wheatley and Sarah Thelwall of the research project 'The Aesthetic and Economic Impact of the Art Market', an investigation into the ways in which the art market shapes artists' careers and public exhibitions (2010-ongoing); *Public Alchemy*, the public programme for the Istanbul Biennial 2013 (co-curated with Fulya Erdemci); and *Tagore, Pedagogy and Contemporary Visual Cultures* (in collaboration with Grant Watson and Institute of International Visual Arts (Iniva), AHRC, 2013–14).

Barbara Steveni

Barbara Steveni conceived and co-founded the Artist Placement Group in 1966. At that time, Steveni and fellow artists recognised their isolation from the real world of industry, commerce and government. APG actively sought to reposition the role of the artist within a wider social context, placing artists within industrial, public and private organisations, and later within government departments. The intention was no longer for the traditional relationship of patronage, but rather to become directly involved in the day-to-day work of the hosting organisations at all levels, including decision-making. This move by artists was to play an important part in the history of conceptual art during the 1960s and 1970s.

In 1968 Group held its first public event, *Industrial Negative Symposium*, at the Mermaid Theatre in London, and in 1971 held an exhibition at the Hayward Gallery entitled *Art & Economics*. This exhibition included examples of APG's Industrial Placements with the British Steel Corporation, Coal Board, Scottish Television, Milton Keynes Development Corporation, and ICI Fibres Ltd, among others. The exhibition also featured a series of discussions on the role of art and artists in these new contexts, held between APG artists and representatives from hosting organisations alongside politicians and educationalists.

Steveni's artistic practice continues through exhibition, panel discussion and performance. Aspects of APG re-emerge through her *I Am An Archive* series of participatory walks, which revisit significant APG Placement sites. Her current work, *Conversations between Ourselves*, documents the largely unrecognised role of women within APG and related art practice of that time.

Gilane Tawadros

Gilane Tawadros is the Chief Executive of DACS. Established by artists for artists, DACS is a not-for-profit visual artists' rights management organisation. Over a period of 30 years, DACS has generated over £67m in revenues for 20,000 artists and is committed to transforming the financial landscape for visual artists. In 2014, DACS launched the *DACS Foundation*, a new charitable arm aimed at making a significant difference in the lives of artists and artists' estates, and *Artimage*, a unique image resource of modern and contemporary art.

She was the founding director of the Institute of International Visual Arts (Iniva) in London, chaired by Professor Stuart Hall, which, over a decade, achieved an international reputation as a ground-breaking cultural agency at the leading edge of artistic and cultural debates nationally and internationally.

She has curated numerous exhibitions, including: *Veil* (New Art Gallery, Walsall; Bluecoat Art Gallery & Open Eye Gallery, Liverpool; Modern Art, Oxford, 2003; and Kulturehuset, Stockholm, 2004), *Fault Lines: Contemporary African Art and Shifting Landscapes*, 50th Venice Biennale (2003) *The Real Me* (Institute of Contemporary Art, London (2005), *Brighton Photo Biennial* (2006), *Alien Nation* (ICA and tour, 2006–7), *Transmission Interrupted* (Modern Art, Oxford, 2009).

She has written extensively on contemporary art. Her books include *Changing States: Contemporary Art and Ideas in an Era of Globalisation* (Iniva, 2004) and *Life is More Important Than Art* (Ostrich, 2007).

She was a board director and then president of the International Foundation of Manifesta (Amsterdam) and serves on the boards of Camden Arts Centre (London), London Film and Video Umbrella, Matt's Gallery and the editorial board of Whitechapel Art Gallery.

Andrew Wheatley

After graduating in Fine Art from St Martin's School of Art in 1986, Andrew Wheatley's peripatetic work in arts administration led him to co-direct the Cabinet Gallery from 1992 when he presented *From Hell*, a two-part show. The formative and eclectic reach of Cabinet variously encompassed exhibitions, readings and performances by Paul Buck, Pierre Guyotard, Jeremy Deller, Elizabeth Peyton, Orphandrift, Pierre Molinier and Jim Shaw. Moving from Brixton in 1999, Martin Creed's *Half the Air in a Given Space* inaugurated Cabinet's Clerkenwell gallery. A second space was opened in 2002 with *TG24*, a display of material drawn from Throbbing Gristle's archive.

Relocating to the historic site of Vauxhall Pleasure Gardens in summer 2015 to occupy a newly designed building, Cabinet will continue to represent an international roster of artists including Ed Atkins, Gillian Carnegie, Marc Chaimowicz, Jay Chung & Q Takeki Maeda, Cosey Fanni Tutti, John Knight, Mark Leckey, Lucy McKenzie, Jim Nutt, Henrik Olesen and more recently, Jana Euler, Richard Kern, James Richards, Anna Blessmann & Peter Saville, as well as the estate of Pierre Klossowski.

Cabinet's curatorial activities at associate commercial galleries and annual trade fairs are complimented by publishing ventures, most recently established under the aegis of its new imprint, Vauxhall & Company. The first publication was an English translation of *The Immortal Adolescent* by Pierre Klossowski.

Throughout his career, Wheatley has periodically acted as an independent consultant in the public sector; he has written arts policy, distributed government funding, assessed multi-million pound lottery applications and developed the UK's first artists' mentoring scheme for the Arts Council.

It would do us all well artists and as people w that without artists th of the other stuff that

Alastair Gentry, Instituted by Artists, June 2012

to remember, as
ho work in the arts,
ere could be none
goes on.

Acknowledgements

We would like to thank Louisa Buck, Alan Freeman, John Kieffer, Keir McGuinness, Courtney J. Martin, Lynda Morris, Andrea Phillips and Andrew Wheatley for their thought-provoking and insightful texts, which open up new ways of thinking about the economy of art, and Sonia Boyce, Jeremy Deller and Barbara Steveni for interrupting the texts with artworks that explore the same theme with highly individual artistic interventions. We are very grateful to Linda Schofield for her thoughtful editing, Stuart Smith and Justine Schuster for their beautiful design, and to Claire Evans and Joanne Milmoe who have guided and supported the development of this book from the very beginning. Thanks also to Paul Hobson and the Contemporary Art Society for collaborating with us on the New Economy of Art debates. *The New Economy of Art* book and accompanying debates have been generously supported by Arts Council England's Grants for the Arts funding, with additional support from University of the Arts London.